Dick Stiles is a retired chartered mechanical engineer who lives in New South Wales, Australia. He has spent most of his working life in the Oil and Gas Industry, having first served in the Royal Navy. The culmination of his career was a two-year spell in Iraq, where he worked as the program manager for the post-invasion reconstruction of the country's oil and gas infrastructure. His time is now taken up with philosophical study, traditional timber boat building, and caring for his grandchildren. This is Dick's first literary publication.

Dick Stiles

OUR FUTURE

Can We Assure Ourselves
That There Is One?

AUSTIN MACAULEY PUBLISHERS™

LONDON * CAMBRIDGE * NEW YORK * SHARJAH

A CIP catalogue record for this title is available from the British Library.

ISBN 9781398432307 (Paperback)
ISBN 9781398432314 (ePub e-book)

www.austinmacauley.com

First Published 2024
Austin Macauley Publishers Ltd®
1 Canada Square
Canary Wharf
London
E14 5AA

To Austin Macauley, the Publishers, for giving me the opportunity to publish what I believe to be a vital and compelling summary of where humanity stands today.

My great friend and fellow philosophical muse, Phil Doley.

Table of Contents

Summary

It was always the intention for Climate Change to take centre stage of this book. However, as it became clear that it was little more than an inevitable product of humankind's practical and psychological evolutionary development, it paved the way for a deeper investigation into these matters. While the consequences of disregarding the phenomena and continuing to conduct 'business as usual' will almost certainly have catastrophic consequences for many parts of the planet, it will be hard to effect the necessary changes to the world's infrastructure and humanity's current behaviours without addressing their personal foibles or more precisely, their pathologies. Rather than simply presenting this conclusion as a 'Fait accompli', the book takes a selective look at those stages of human history which have had the biggest influence on society today with a view to offering both explanation and possible solution. This begins with Homo Sapiens as a hunter/gatherer and then progresses to the behaviours of the larger groups of humanity as they spread across the globe, the Ancient Greek Philosophers, the birth and rise of Christianity and the early challenge it faced from Muslimism, the Age of Enlightenment, the Industrial Revolution, the two World Wars and concludes with the material and communication explosion/revolution that has taken place since then. By piecing these events together, an entirely plausible explanation is presented as to how humanity has reached this point in its history. With the help of a significant input from both ancient and modern philosophy, the behaviours necessary to close the glaring gaps in humankind's evolutionary history are explored and the mechanism which will ensure the successful changes necessary to arrest Global Warming is teased out. Some of the successes the world can claim to date are recorded as well as the formidable technical challenges that must still be met and overcome. On the surface, the solution is straightforward. However, its universal adoption will be far more difficult. While it is too late to effect a complete change and reversal of the consequences that are already apparent or which have been set in train, the opportunity remains whereby the more severe impacts predicted can be ameliorated and a familiar model of earthly existence, most probably still with some notable differences compared with the present day, can prevail.

Because the solution presented relies on each and every member of the human race playing their part and has also been based on the continuation of the noteworthy measure of international tolerance shown in the last 20 or 30 years, particularly between the dominant nations of the world, the invasion of Ukraine by Russia in late February 2022, has to some extent, derailed the level of optimism associated with the predicted outcomes. Sadly, the alarming pathologies which have been exposed have suggested a dramatic regression to a level not seen since the Second World War. There is some tragic irony in the juxtaposition of this and Climate Change as Russia has created a background story to justify its invasion which lays the blame on Ukraine for allowing the 'Nazification' of its country which Russia is trying to cleanse. World opinion is split on the veracity of this story but consensus is firmly on the side of Ukraine's complete dismissal of it. The loudest and most aggressive cry coming from the 'Climate Activists' is one of blame, this time pointing at governments, industry and individuals for polluting the planet. Both are the result of humanity's urge to make up stories and to lay blame on others to remove the focus on their own actions. A very substantial part of minimising the effects of Climate Change lies with humankind's ability to acknowledge that each and every one of us is responsible for it and that without this, there is little hope for an effective global solution.

Forward

Is material wealth more important than cognitive and spiritual wealth? Is it better to strive for the material comforts that come with possession or the peace and equilibrium that is the product of practising meaningful empathetic, compassionate and non-judgemental behaviour? Is it inevitable that it is only possible to pursue one of these choices but not both? Is there a day or even just an hour that goes by during that day when a member of the human race manages not to round on another individual or group laying the finger of blame for some action, behaviour or inaction? These are the stark, invariably unpleasant traits of today's world societies. They are not all being practised everywhere at the same level or intensity, perhaps unsurprisingly the more wealthy and materially abundant a society has become, the more widespread the behaviour. Does any of this matter? Are these references to spiritual behaviour simply archaic leftovers from a world once dominated by religion? Or are they the markers of a civilisation in serious and perhaps irreversible decline? And where does Climate Change fit amongst all this?

Chapter One
Utopia, Dystopia and Disaster movies

Looking back over the last 120 years, the question of humanity's future has been addressed both directly and circuitously by innumerable sages, philosophers, spiritualists, authors, film makers, social commentators and intense undergraduate debating societies throughout the western world. Both utopian and dystopian books have been written, some to great effect. Many of them have claimed a place in literature's halls of fame. Films have been made either based on the books or have had their own dramatic screenplay especially created, often to suit the medium itself. Strangely, society grasps these productions with both hands and invariably lauds their content. They portray the future in a variety of ways but they usually don't conclude with cataclysmic and total destruction. In the case of the many films produced, this is probably driven by the producer wanting to leave the door open for a sequel! But perhaps there is something more fundamental to account for this. Certainly, human beings like to frighten themselves with horror stories but they are usually seen for what they are, either as a simple means of escapism or a device to stimulate the sometimes underworked imagination. The more enduring and thought provoking novels have tended to focus on the type of world that develops, its governing structure and the consequential living conditions being experienced by future generations. George Orwell[1], the author of the dystopian novel *1984* was an acknowledged social commentator of the time and it was entirely fitting that he should project his thoughts on a possible future society in such a novel. The book is disturbing because the world it describes is one of brutal authoritarian rule. The origin of the character used by reality television today, *Big Brother* was introduced by Orwell. Whereas in the television shows, the character is authoritarian and supposedly 'all-seeing', it is little more than a pantomime villain compared with Orwell's chilling description of his powers over every member of society. As this was written some 40 years before the arrival of the internet and the associated social media, its prescience is alarming. Ray Bradbury's[2] book *Fahrenheit 451* foretells of a disturbing future, basing it on a society being led by an authoritarian establishment that has responded to their own anxieties concerning the written word. Books are banned, outlawed and destroyed wherever they appear, their owners being appropriately punished, 451 degrees Fahrenheit being the temperature at which paper combusts spontaneously. The earth's history is thus suitably manipulated to suit the whim of the controlling world authority and leaving a society to conduct its business in a perpetual state of anxiety. Other future looking works have concentrated more on the development of science and technology. These have tended to populate the 'Science Fiction' genre, which by its very nature is futuristic.

There is no shortage of literary material that takes one small element of society and builds a futuristic story around it. Author Kazuo Ishiguro's[3] novel *Never let me go* is based on the concept of harvesting human body parts for transplant. This is a grim concept but deals with the possibility that humanity's current grip on medical ethics is relaxed. It does not explore the broader ramifications of such an environment existing, simply leaving that to the reader's imagination. In his novel *Klara and the sun*, Ishiguro paints a picture of humanity having decided to use its technology advancement to provide companions for troubled single children in the form of robots. These companions are highly developed technically so that they can mimic a human physically and to some extent, mentally but their programming causes them to struggle with the more complex areas of human emotion. They also have a short 'life span', seemingly not much longer than the average duration of adolescence. Ishiguro paints his concept into a future world space where, by inference much has happened to government and society but the same requirements to have partners, marry, procreate, work, entertain and be entertained are still very much in evidence. A seemingly elitist process is alluded to whereby early adolescents are given the opportunity to undergo some sort of neurological enhancement which will elevate their status as adults. The consequential societal division that such a process creates is one of the enduring themes in the book. Arrival at this point in history appears to have been the result, at least in part of earlier war(s). Although not explicitly discussed there is an overwhelming sense of authoritarian control. An ingenious theme runs through the book which offers the reader a possible cause for optimism and that is the relationship that Klara appears to have with the sun. On the one hand, this could be dismissed as being little more than an aberration in the algorithms that control her, while on the other hand it could be suggestive of some form of union between and recognition of nature by artificial intelligence. Interestingly, this is the inverse of the theme presented by James Lovelock[4] in his book *Novacene* which was published in 2019 and deals with his view of the most likely outcome of the integration of AI with humanity. In it, he sees humankind's survival being largely conditional on its usefulness in continuing to connect with nature, something AI may require help with.

Aldos Huxley's[5] *Brave New World*, written in 1932 focused on the potential de-humanising aspects of material and scientific advancement. Considering the year it was published, it was a radical picture. His world no longer required adults to procreate, this process and the subsequent nurturing of children being performed by the state in purpose made facilities. Sex was simply for enjoyment and freely available to anyone who wished to partake of it. It had none of the long held taboos of the late nineteenth and early twentieth century associated with it. Government appeared to be little more than an extension of industry. There was wide use of drugs to help control the mood of the populace and even create 'artificial holidays' if the subject's diagnosis demanded it. Alongside but very much outside the central mass of society, living in an artificially stimulated heavily material based environment, there were groups of 'savages', the name given to those humans that had somehow missed the massive upheavals which had created the 'Brave New World'. These savages clung to an older way of life, to literature and poetry but were complete outcasts. Where the two cultures crossed, it was fair game for the savages to become both physical and psychological targets.

There have been innumerable sorties into the future both in literature and cinematography. It is reasonable to postulate that the work by the four authors described above has been based on a critical examination of the societies they were or are still living in, their findings then being projected into a future world with suitable modification or embellishment. While the five books are most certainly all works of fiction, there are some disturbing themes developed in each one which continue to give food for thought even 90 years later.

The films that have been produced, some based on original books, others having had their own screenplay written from scratch tend to focus on the catastrophic. Typically, they portray a world dealing with the after-effects of a meteorite strike, floods of Biblical proportion, huge volcanic activity, pandemics or alien invasion. There doesn't seem to be much appetite for tracing any sort of societal degradation as a root cause of a major catastrophe. The film *Soylent Green*[6] released in 1973 does take a slightly different approach. It depicts a future world corrupted by materialism and run by big business corporations that are at odds with their fellow citizens, such that rioting in the streets is a daily event. Food is scarce and the population is being forced to sustain itself by encouraging euthanasia amongst its elderly and then using their earthly remains in the heavily regulated food chain. The film was certainly designed to shock!

More recently, there has been another futuristic 'Disaster Movie' released called *Don't look up*[7]. Once again, the theme is imminent catastrophe, this time to be caused by a meteorite striking the earth. The final impact is not part of the film but the audience is left with little doubt that it will happen, and the combined efforts of the world's scientists and engineers have been less than adequate to save the bulk of humankind. Only a few of the chosen elite are given the vaguest semblance of a chance as they board a craft bound for a 'Galaxy far, far away'. Whether they make it is moot. Running through the fabric of the storyline is the mischief that is being created by the media. This has struck a chord with audiences around the world because it is easy to draw a very real comparison between the less than honourable and honest behaviour displayed in the movie and the way in which the media are being seen to operate in today's real world. This may be a harsh criticism based on a generalised view of matters but it is not without merit.

Of course, the radical alteration of our planet Earth caused by flood, meteorite strike, or massive volcanic activity to name a few, could result in it no longer being able to sustain human life. This has spawned the *Don't look up* closing scenario to which, incidentally the script writers have no exclusive rights. Escape to another planet is not a new theme. The achievability of such a move has been 'talked up' not only by the creators of fiction books and film scripts but also, rather sadly by elements of the scientific and engineering communities of the world. The search for another Earth or 'Goldilocks Planet', one that is not too hot and not too cold, just like the Baby Bear's porridge, has been going on for a long time and the probability of finding one, never mind being able to travel there in a human life time is astronomically slim. As for the more recent news of plans to set up some sort of colony on the Moon and then Mars is certainly exciting and is reminiscent of the determination, ingenuity and extraordinary bravery shown by the earthly explorers of the last four or five centuries.

However, with humanity's current grasp of the ways of converting naturally occurring and readily available energy into a useful medium to sustain life, the probability of that scenario being realised is on a par or even lower than finding the right bowl of porridge. Despite these small limiting practicalities, it does add substance to humankind's optimism even if it is misplaced.

The other 'end of humanity' scenario is nuclear war. This has been extant as a real threat since the 1950s. The book written by Nevil Shute[8], published in 1957 and the subsequent film first screened in 1959 both entitled *On the Beach*, recount the final months and days on planet earth through the eyes of the last of the survivors of a nuclear war. The Cold War between the Soviet Union and the Western Allies was gathering momentum at that time and the trauma experienced by Japan as a result of the two Atomic Bombs dropped on Hiroshima and Nagasaki in 1945 was still very raw and visible to the rest of the world. The film had a profound effect on people when it was first released but that effect has not diminished with time. Today, philosopher, historian and author Yuval Hariri, regards nuclear war as one of the greatest risks facing humankind. He is not alone.

Of course, large elements of humanity enjoy being frightened which is why stories which have this effect continue to be told, written down, made into films, or acted out on the stage. There seems to be no limit to the collective appetite. But what happens when humanity is faced with a real and present threat? First of all, can it actually identify it? If it manages to do this, will a majority collective response be possible or will a lack of understanding, a plethora of publicly available misinformation, simple denial or more complex conspiracy theories surrounding its veracity prevail? Will vested interest override common sense because the potential loss of wealth and economic stability go hand in hand with any of the proposed solutions to avert disaster? The movies tend to just concentrate on the disasters themselves. After all, it makes good cinematography. The ones that are averted are usually managed by an elite few. They may have their token detractors in the storyline but they are not really a force to be taken too seriously by the heroes of the day. In short, it seems that the stories we tell ourselves and which we enjoy listening to, watching or reading are simple ones. There is an issue, there is a solution, there are a trusty band of heroes to prosecute that solution, there are the inevitable bad guys and there is a culminating scene where the misery continues, as in Soylent Green, or the world is saved.

So, where does Global Warming or Climate Change fit into this picture? It is, after all supposed to be a real and present threat to humanity. There have been myriad specialist engineers, scientists, environmentalists, whole world renowned institutions, and a few sovereign governments shouting about it over the last 30 years but has any of it gained any real traction with those elements of humanity that have the power, the commitment, the wisdom, and the environmental empathy to do something about it? If it has, then progress towards a solution that will either mitigate or remove the anticipated consequences seems modest at best. Meanwhile, a huge level of anxiety has been seen to be building throughout the world, particularly amongst the younger generations. Has this anxiety been generated solely by the level and extent of current media coverage, both mainstream and social, or has its intensity been heightened by the very images that humanity has seemingly enjoyed exposing itself to over the last hundred odd years?

Chapter Two
The Elephant in the Room

The plan here is not to add to the already overwhelming volume of data supporting the concept of Climate Change but rather to explore the possibility of any tangible connection between it and humanity's obsession with its future. What is 'on offer' from Climate Change is not in the same league as a large meteorite crashing into Earth as happened towards the end of the Jurassic Geological Period and which is assumed to have put paid to the dinosaur, nor is it Armageddon caused by a massive nuclear war waged between earthly superpowers, the results of which were so starkly imagined by Nevil Shute. These events would almost certainly destroy the atmosphere on which most sentient life forms depend and it would be unlikely to recover until well after humanity had become extinct. No, it is much more subtle than that, insidious even. In its unchecked form, current measured trends suggest that the Earth will suffer an increase in its mean (Or average) temperature of one or two degrees Celsius over the next 30 years[1]. That will have an impact on many elements of life on Earth although it is highly improbable that it would overwhelm humans as an animal species on its own. But it is only the short-term picture which experts state is unavoidable if humanity continues to live, work and play as it has done over the last few decades. The longer term picture, well into the twenty-second century, will not only depend on how the present threat is dealt with, but also on whether the relatively small changes associated with it, lead to further stimulation of the Earth's climate causing positive or negative feed-back loops either of which could cause wild temperature variations. Under this scenario, the future is less certain.

Humankind has made a study of its planet Earth over several thousand years. In the last three hundred years, the knowledge and measured data being garnered by such studies has risen exponentially. It is well documented from geological investigations that the Earth has experienced significant changes in temperature over its life sustaining years. There have been Ice Ages, sea level rises and falls and wild temperature swings. It is these events that have helped to shape the Earth as it is today. Despite humanity's feelings of comfortable constancy when viewing its surroundings, things are in a perpetual state of flux but this is a concept which is not grasped easily. The sea level doesn't appear to change when viewed with the naked eye except for tidal variations which are now well understood and can be predicted with a high level of accuracy and repeatability. One summer feels much like the last. Of course, summers were always dryer and hotter when viewed with hindsight and a large dose of nostalgia but subjective observation is of little value over the short timeframe prescribed by the life of a human being. The frequency and intensity of bad weather is another yardstick by which comparisons can be made but without rigorous data collection it is as subjective as the comparisons drawn from memory over the heat or dryness of preceding summers. So it is not surprising that when national and international alarm bells are being rung over the consequences of Climate Change, the first response from humans is one of scepticism or outright dismissal. There are no meteorite tracks being plotted daily by the media showing an eventual impact with earth. If sea level is rising or has risen in the last 50 years, it is only being measured in millimetres and that is hardly dramatic unless it is viewed by a mid-ocean islander living on a land mass which is literally only inches above sea level. The changes in weather patterns and intensity may well be there but this is the stuff of a hysterical prone mainstream media vying for more drama by the day and so its relevance is easily denied. Despite all the evidence being marshalled and presented to everyone who cares to read about it, the situation doesn't appear to have caught the average human being's imagination in the same way that a disaster movie does. A dystopian future remains firmly locked away in the pages of books and the images of movies. Humanity, it would seem, does not need to worry about such matters. But maybe that's not really surprising because the tangible consequences of Climate Change are still some way off and are unlikely to be observed and felt by either John or Jane Doe in the next 20 years. However, what is more likely to be experienced is the social fallout which could well be seen between the different factions of human society reacting to the constant cranking up of anxiety levels if nothing is being seen to be done by those who have been identified as being most responsible.

As is invariably the case with human behaviour, if a problem has been identified that affects others then someone is responsible for creating it, someone or some group of humanity must take the blame. This is a sad reaction but is entirely in keeping with the behavioural norms that can be observed throughout Western society in particular. While there is a great deal of science associated with the modelling of the Earth's climate, an enormous amount of data supporting it and some highly complex relationships between the myriad elements that go together to make up the overall model, it has been made very clear that the excessive amounts of carbon dioxide finding its way into the Earth's atmosphere as a result of human activities is a major contributor to the looming changes. To a very vocal minority, this alone is enough to call-out all the industries who discharge carbon dioxide into the atmosphere as a consequence of their daily operations. They must take the blame and they must fix it! But just as the Climate Change model is inordinately complex and interdependent on so many different input variables so too is the practical societal environment that the discharging industries are a part of. If some all-powerful human deity was to demand that everything emitting carbon dioxide was to cease operating at midnight tonight, then it would generate the most spectacular scenario for a disaster movie imaginable. Instantaneously, there would be no power to millions and millions of towns and cities around the world. Hospitals would cease to function. There would be no heating and cooling, no transport by land, sea or air, no distribution of food, goods or fuel, no more construction or repair of infrastructure, no more manufacturing to list but a few of the immediate consequences. In a very short period, there would be total anarchy as people were forced to do whatever they could to provide for themselves and their families. Any prospect of recovery from such a scenario would be remote. Fortunately, this is highly unlikely to develop but rather ironically, a desire to avoid such an outcome is not the main reason why such drastic measures are unlikely to be taken. The reason for this lies in the complexity and interdependence of today's human society together with the primary drivers that developed it in the first place, and which continue to ensure its operation.

Thomas Newcomen[2], a metal worker born in Dartmouth in the West of England in 1664 is generally regarded as being one of the first clearly identifiable figures responsible for the successful mechanisation of a process which had hitherto been carried out by humans or animals. His was the first steam driven pump designed to operate at atmospheric pressure. It was conceived in 1712 to assist with the removal of ground water that was frustrating the efforts of tin miners in Cornwall to extract all the available ore from each mine, although most of the pumps built to his design ended up being used in the mines in England's Midlands. Like many early mechanical inventions, it owes its origins to human ingenuity which had been directed at a problem in order to speed up an operation, make it less burdensome for the human or animal tasked with carrying it out, or extend the useful life of something like a mine which was being overwhelmed by flooding. In turn, these imperatives resulted in relieving humanity of the need to perform so much repetitive physical work which would have extended working lives, eased the physical burden and kept employment going in areas where environmental conditions were overly challenging. Of course, the drivers were not all altruistic by any means. It was seen very quickly that machines could improve production times, volumes and later the quality of the produced article which would lead to the generation of more wealth for the owners. Not only was this the birth of the Industrial Revolution but also of Capitalism.

There are plenty of social histories which track the course of the Industrial Revolution. For some, it caused great hardship, while for others, it offered the chance of employment, an income and the opportunity to improve living standards and quality of life. There were many setbacks, some brought about by accidents which often occurred in nascent industries trying to run before they could walk, a feature of industrialised nations to this day. There was massive exploitation of the workforce in terms of the hours that were worked and the conditions that had to be endured. The abuse of children was widespread. Often, they were expected to carry out the job of an adult, regardless of the damage it was doing to their still developing bodies for a fraction of the wage, or they were used because their size allowed them access to horrifically cramped positions underneath or behind machines or down mines. Education was following close on the heels of industry but it was many years before society gave it the authority to keep children out of the workforce. Meanwhile, the entrepreneurs, the company owners, the managers and the opportunists were all increasing their wealth, their comforts and their overall quality of life. For many countries, this is now largely a historical picture but for others this remains a very accurate snapshot of modern life.

If life in England in 1712 is compared with life there today, 310 years later, the differences are staggering. But if the comparison is made in the other direction, 2000 years earlier and with another part of the globe which was far more developed than England, namely Greece, then the differences are nothing like as pronounced. This is because humanity's technical and manufacturing advances suddenly exploded at the beginning of the eighteenth century. The ancient civilisations had made many extraordinary discoveries and deductions, especially when considering the limited resources that were available at that time. But the harnessing of an energy source, the transfer of that form of energy to another form which could then be used to perform effectively endless repetitive work was something the Ancients had toyed with but for a variety of reasons, had either not been able to or had not wanted to realise the potential. Newcomen and his successors had no such reticence. The pressure had certainly been building in the previous few centuries before Newcomen was born with a raft of great scientific discoveries but it was almost as if the underlying theories needed to be teased out and understood before humankind's ingenuity could be let loose. When it was, not only countless inventions were conceived, designed, built and put into large scale production but with them came their availability to an ever-increasing percentage of the world, first in the more developed nations but quickly spreading to the entire planet. And with that growth, came the sense of entitlement which drove expectation, participation and ownership in all the wizardry associated with modern society ever forward. Today, in the parts of the world that have benefitted first from the spoils of the Industrial Revolution, everyone expects to be able to live in a home, heat it, cool it and light it, have a constant supply of fresh water, have odourless sewage disposal and a waste collection service, buy food of their choice year around without having to suffer from seasonal availability constraints, participate in the constant acquisition of labour-saving devices and myriad consumer items, own a car, travel around the country or further afield on a system of roads for work or leisure, travel on a rail network that weaves a country's towns and cities into a hugely valuable web of connectivity, be cared for by a health system, be kept safe by a police force, fly to other parts of the country or world in high speed jet propelled aircraft, stay constantly connected to and participate in social media and the internet, be provided with instantaneous news of events taking place anywhere around the world at any time, enjoy free or heavily subsidised education, and be supported by state sponsored welfare should the need arise. In countries where the industrial progress has been slower, not all of these entitlements are shared equally amongst the population but because of communication and worldwide connectivity, they are already on the collective 'wish list' and are a very clear goal.

All of these entitlements can be met in a developed country provided that there is an adequate and environmentally acceptable supply of useable energy together with a government establishment that recognises and supports countrywide material suffrage.

In developing countries, the picture is not quite so clear. While they may benefit from an even-handed democratic leadership, the associated practicalities of delivery, especially over wide and often inhospitable land masses to a significant sized population can slow universal delivery dramatically. However, where the leadership of a country is authoritarian or dictatorial then the physical challenges are compounded, the problems balloon and the chances of countrywide success diminish accordingly.

As humankind has advanced its technologies for converting energy and providing it in a useful form to its peoples, developed more and more sophisticated transportation systems, conceived and improved its written and spoken communication with one another to a point unimaginable a hundred years ago, advanced its knowledge, use and availability of medicine and made so much of the trappings of capitalism within the grasp of millions, the sentiment that has driven all this has remained fundamentally self-serving. Engineers and scientists work on new discoveries, improving existing facilities, making things more accessible, faster, cleaner, easier to use or more exciting to look at in order to make human lives more tolerable. This goes hand in glove with increasing production, having more things to offer more people to purchase thereby increasing and enhancing employment and wealth. These are the elemental drivers behind capitalism. As an economic and societal model, it has many detractors. However, up to this point in humanity's evolution it is hard to point to a system that has delivered anything remotely approaching the advancements and associated benefits that are enjoyed because of it.

In what is an incredibly short space of evolutionary time, humankind has now been made aware of a new threat to its seemingly stable and comfortable existence on planet Earth. Furthermore, there is ample evidence being presented that suggests that the very development and prosperity it has and continues to enjoy, is in no small way responsible for this threat. In order to address it, there is an understanding that there needs to be wholesale change. The great bulk of the energy conversion process that is used to drive the economies of the world needs to be replaced and that replacement or modification, once accepted as being necessary, will require a dramatic shift in paradigms that currently prevail across both industry and society. It will require enormous modification of equipment, plant, machinery, utilities, transportation, the list goes on, for it to be enacted. There will be colossal costs associated with it and potentially considerable disruption to employment and lifestyles. The irony is that much of what is required happens on a daily basis anyway, perhaps not as fast but as a part of the ever advancing cycle of capitalism. The differences between the evolutionary changes associated with the pursuit of capitalism and the response to Climate Change lie in the drivers. In the former case, they have been extant for most of the industrial revolution in some form or another, while in the latter case they are quite new, less tangible and severely exposed to ridicule and even dismissal. The changes are required, humanity is told because the way things are done at the moment is upsetting planet Earth profoundly, changing its relatively stable temperature profile by degrading its atmosphere, causing more of its freshwater reserves trapped in solid form to be released into the oceans, disrupting the pattern and intensity of the weather systems that prevail around the planet and abusing and degrading the natural environment with waste and pollution. For some, the evidence for all this is incontrovertible and action needs to be taken immediately while for others it may or may not be significant but regardless of any action designed to resolve or at least mitigate matters, it is just simply too inconvenient and offensive to contemplate.

In order to address the principal issue, that of global temperature rise it has been determined that a drastic reduction in the amount of Greenhouse gas generated and released by humankind must be achieved. Humanity, it seems has been disturbing the natural balance of the mix of gases that make up the atmosphere by adding excessive amounts of carbon dioxide and methane, both largely the result of the industrialisation that has taken place over the last three hundred years. Both of these gases are normal constituent parts of the atmosphere, occurring quite naturally within the environment. However, a noteworthy increase in global temperature has already been attributed to the now established imbalance, and if this imbalance is to be corrected and temperature rise limited, then it is essential that further human generated releases must either be stopped completely or be reduced dramatically. While methane is a much more potent Greenhouse gas when compared with carbon dioxide, its global volumetric release is very much smaller. It will be important to put controls in place to deal with it but the impact of such controls on society will be less significant. However, carbon dioxide is another matter. It is a by-product of the majority of the industries that serve humankind and the major emissions come from power plants, those facilities that convert one energy form to another so that it is convenient for use in the home or industry. More specifically, it is those plants that burn fossil fuels to boil water to produce steam which is then pressurised to drive a turbine which in turn drives a generator that converts its rotational kinetic energy into electricity. This electricity is then transmitted across a complex network of cables and wires to all the users who will benefit from it to drive machinery, power factories and food processing facilities, run railways, pump water or sewage, light streets, heat, cool and light places of work and homes, drive domestic appliances, run computers and entire communication networks, charge innumerable devices, run hospital equipment and services, to name but a few of those elements of daily life that rely on electrical power. The offending fossil fuels vary in form. The main ones are coal, oil and gas. Interestingly, they are all the product of a naturally occurring earthly process of plant growth, death, decomposition, burial, compression and change of state, all happening over an extended time period. The youngest product is coal. It has been mined for hundreds of years. The intensity of the mining process increased dramatically with the advent of the Industrial Revolution. Although John Newcomen burnt wood to heat his water to make steam to drive his pump, his successors burnt coal to achieve the same ends. Not only is coal burnt to heat water to make steam to turn a turbine, it is also possible to process it to make 'Town Gas', the predecessor to natural gas. The gas stoves and lighting in the homes of the late nineteenth and early twentieth century were all fuelled by Town Gas, as were the streetlights. Coal or more particularly a derivative, coke is also a fundamental component of the steel manufacturing process.

Oil and natural gas are the older citizens of the biomass metamorphosis. They are usually found together although not always and have been successfully extracted, stabilised and refined for well over a hundred years. The industries and transport systems of the twentieth and twenty-first centuries have developed, grown and prospered on the back of these resources. Not only could electrical power be produced by burning them as with coal but they also gave birth to an entire process industry by providing the feedstock for the production of plastics, laminates, fertiliser and a host of different chemicals. The oil has powered the transport systems of the world including aircraft, ships, cars, trucks and railway engines and has facilitated their rapid development from the basic models of the late nineteenth century to the sophisticated machinery that is taken for granted today.

The number and distribution of fossil fuel powered electrical generation facilities throughout the world is vast and complex. They range in size from the modest, capable of supplying power to a few thousand homes, to the gargantuan, designed to supply hundreds of thousands of homes and industries. Their locations are usually closely tied to the market they are supplying but they also need to reflect the source of their feedstock, be it oil, gas or coal. Because these facilities or plants have been acknowledged as such a fundamental and essential part of humankind's existence, their intrusion on the environment, whether simply because of their sheer size or more importantly because of the emission of atmospheric and environmental pollutants, has been regarded as an inevitability associated with modern living. In turn, the provision of fuel to run them has been accepted both by the providers of that fuel and the plant operators alike. For those countries fortunate enough to have an abundance of easily extractable fossil fuels, the ability to extract, sell and transport them across the globe to those countries less well blessed has resulted in both supplier and receiver being able to grow their respective economies, provide employment for their citizens and enhance their quality of living. The interdependence of supply and consumption and the imperative of its permanence, especially where power generation is concerned, has resulted in a web of commercial arrangements being woven across the globe which now sustains the livelihoods and the wellbeing of millions if not billions of people.

In like manner, the other industries and facilities that have sprouted around the world on the back of the Industrial Revolution are equally complex and interdependent on partners, suppliers, consumers and the 200 odd governments that establish the rules and guidelines by which sovereign states abide. Historically, if change has taken place within any one of these industries or supporting facilities such as power generation, then the process of change has been gradual and almost always driven by the need, perceived or otherwise, to improve the efficiency of the process being changed, reduce its cost, make it less dependent on manual labour or intervention, upgrade or replace a process or system which has become obsolete or inefficient compared with the technology of the day and thereby improve matters for all those who are either directly or indirectly affected by those industries or facilities. Simply put, it is the practical evolution and development of those same set of drivers to which Newcomen was responding back in the late seventeenth century. However, the response that is now needed to minimise the effects of Climate Change cannot rely on these drivers. They pushed humanity forward because a smarter, cleaner, less noisy, more efficient, more modern, more affordable process or object was worth striving for. The results were tangible. The products could be sat on, driven faster, operated with less physical effort, switched on and off with the press of a button or a voice command. In stark contrast, the effort and upset that will result from the changes required to curb the threatened rise in temperature will have no such tangible results and the drivers that have been behind the initiation and execution of change over the last 300 years will seem completely absent. Instead, they must be replaced by a single imperative, to stop what is being done and has been done to sustain the world for as long as the last three or four generations can remember and replace it with a different solution which will not only be extraordinarily challenging to put into effect right across the globe within a very short space of time but will be disruptive, expensive, and to many, not even necessary.

If the original drivers behind the Industrial Revolution are as real as is suggested, then maybe they can be reengaged. In doing so, it may also be possible to open up a path which will lead to more connectivity between humanity and its environment. While the greater challenge facing humankind is the practical adaptation or replacement of systems across the entire breadth of worldwide industry, the greatest challenge must be the elevation of human thought and behaviour to fully embrace its relationship with nature and the environment of which it is such an important part.

Chapter Three
Some of the Practical Solutions

It is evident from the previous chapter that humankind has a lot to think about and then even more to do if it wants to respond to the considerable challenges that threaten the stability of the Earth and its climate. The Earth is extremely old which is something that can be very difficult to grasp[1]. If its age, as determined by scientific investigation is represented as one 365-day year and we are currently enjoying the 1st of January of the following New Year, then according to that scale, humanity didn't arrive on the planet in its earliest hunter-gatherer form until 11:30 pm on the 31 December. That's a very short space of time in the overall scheme of things, and quite a graspable concept compared with the two hundred thousand years that those thirty minutes represent. Just to put that into sharper focus, dinosaurs occupied Earth for something approaching 30 million years or 150 times as long as humans have to date. The damage that appears to have been done by humans in terms of upsetting the stability of the climate might have had its roots in some of the ancient civilisations of between two and five thousand years ago but it has really only been possible to observe and measure this damage over the last hundred years; that is 0.9 seconds on the 365-day cosmic clock. To have caused such apparent mischief in such an incredibly short space of cosmic time is nothing short of heinous. If the population of the world isn't shocked into corrective action by the starkness of these figures, then there is clearly not an ounce of understanding or empathy for the environment that has sustained it for its short time on Earth.

So, what is needed? Firstly, action globally and with every nation in concert; secondly, philosophical change.

Effective action by one or several countries is eminently achievable as has been demonstrated in humanity's brief history when countries or societies have been challenged by and have overcome overwhelming odds either presented by natural phenomena or, in the case of war by apparent kindred nations. However, there is little or no historical evidence of humanity's ability to work together harmoniously for a common cause. Perhaps the last two years dealing with the Covid-19 pandemic have shed some positive light on matters but realistically it has been more a case of individual countries working to save the skins of their own people. The fact that each country has recognised a common threat and responded in a similar fashion is the only linkage. The desire shown by the wealthier and more developed countries to assist others less fortunate than themselves has been either largely absent or minimal at best. This observed pattern of behaviour surrounding the pandemic sheds light on the second action that is needed, philosophical change. To summarise what is required is straightforward but to encourage and cause its adoption across a large swathe of unenlightened humanity could be light years away.

The matter of power generation has taken centre stage in much of the national and international discussion to date. This is hardly surprising given its significance as presented in the previous chapter. The media has been fulsome in its coverage of 'Alternative renewable energy' for many years. Governments have clutched at the latest percentages achieved of power generated by 'Renewable sources' in order to demonstrate their commitment to a real and tangible response to Climate Change. There is no doubt that progress is being made to shift the global emphasis from fossil fuel to renewable sources. However, there are some very fundamental issues for which humanity has yet to determine a practical, sustainable and agreeable solution. Fossil fuels have provided the vast bulk of the energy that has been required to develop the world to the point it has reached today. To design, engineer, construct, and bring into global operation alternative energy sources and to integrate them with all the existing production and infrastructure on which the world population depends is a task of Herculean proportion. Even the very necessary process of achieving global consensus on the content, direction and timing of a project of this magnitude is a colossal undertaking which has no precedent.

Fundamental to all electrical power generation and distribution systems is the inbuilt ability to cope with a fluctuating demand. In the most obvious situation, there is less electricity being used at night compared with the daytime. What is perhaps less obvious are the fluctuations caused by weather, variable industrial demand and failures within the generation and distribution systems themselves which must be covered. Most generators relying on the burning of fossil fuels for their driving energy source are able to adjust their outputs up and down to suit demand. Systems also benefit from multiple power plants so that smaller generators can be brought online in times of high demand and shut down again when the peak requirement has passed. Because of this inbuilt flexibility, the matter of short or medium term storage of electricity has never really needed to be addressed. However, when generation is fuelled by an energy source other than the heat provided by the burning of fuel, such as wind, sunshine, tidal or wave power then there is an obvious issue when the sun doesn't shine, or the wind doesn't blow. Vast arrays of solar panels stretching across the world's deserts are a heartening sight when it is realised that they are producing the equivalent of a massively polluting coal burning power station with absolutely no release of damaging Greenhouse gas but what happens to the industries that are receiving their power from these giant solar arrays when darkness descends? They will either be forced to shut production down, something which is not possible if their plant is designed to run continuously or draw their power from an alternative source. Much has been made of the use of batteries to store generated electricity and the concept is admirable. In simple terms, when the wind blows and the sun shines the power stations produce as much electricity as they can, storing the surplus power in banks of batteries which can then be discharged into the grid when generation is not possible. The principal is sound but the reality is wanting. Current battery technology is not able to produce such a system. It may be able to in the future but at present, the volume of energy requiring to be stored and the battery discharge rates necessary to be of any practical use to industry simply cannot be achieved. In addition, the availability of the more exotic raw materials necessary to manufacture the batteries is limited, their design life is relatively short, and the costs involved with manufacture, distribution, and end of life disposal and recycling are prohibitive.

Some renewable mediums are more constant such as tidal power and to a lesser extent, wave power. Generators using these mediums are in the process of translating from prototype units to small size full production ones which will be connected to the local electricity grid. This is very encouraging but their electrical generation capacity, necessary location and anticipated design life mean that they will need to be installed in huge numbers before they are able to replace the power generated in a single large fossil fuelled power station. However, one renewable source has been quietly and relatively unobtrusively storing night-time generation for many years, Hydro-electric power. This is sometimes referred to as Pumped Hydro Energy Storage (PHES)[2]. In particular, it relates to power stations which rely on what is essentially a static body of water above them contained in a lake or reservoir. High levels of generation take place during the day to meet the domestic and industrial demand but when that demand falls at night, the water flow rate is kept the same and the surplus power being generated is used to run pumps that return the water to the lake or reservoir thus re-stocking the potential energy of the original water source. Not all Hydro-electric power stations can be operated in this manner but wherever possible and assuming that the environmental intrusion caused by the additional plant necessary is acceptable, they should be encouraged.

There are other storage systems being developed. These include Thermo-Mechanical Energy Storage (TMES[3]) and Compressed Air Energy Storage (CAES[4]). They rely on the basic laws of thermodynamics and, for optimal output, a particular geological environment. Looking at CAES first, it works by using surplus electrical power to compress air. This air can then be stored in pressure vessels or in subterranean cavernous structures, possibly those previously containing hydrocarbons that have been depleted. When the primary source of power for generation is not available, the compressed air can be released and used as a driver for generation. Issues with heating and cooling of the air during compression and decompression can be dealt with to enhance the overall efficiency. Costs of generating in this way compare very favourably with PHES which has been used for many years. Thermo Mechanical Energy Storage as its name suggests, uses the excess power not required to supply the grid to heat other mediums such as water, oils or molten salts. The heat held in the medium can be released at a later time and used to power further generation.

There is every reason to be optimistic about energy storage which will be essential to enhance the efficacy of electrical generation powered by renewable sources if they are to replace the current fossil fuel burning power plants. However, much of the development surrounding the necessary plant is in its infancy. It will need to go through prototype development and testing first. Further proving of the technology will follow with the construction, operation and integration of smaller operational plants. Depending on the success of these phases, only then will it be possible to scale the whole process up to a size that will be capable of replacing the massive fossil fuel burning units that are presently relied upon worldwide. Timelines for turning an engineering or manufacturing process 'New idea' into a large, reliable and investment suitable reality are seldom less than ten years and often considerably longer. There is also the question of the very adoption of some of these measures being highly controversial because of the perceived or actual environmental disturbance. Many PHES proposals have been rejected on these grounds over the last 50 years, some involving the modification of existing power stations while others have been with proposed new projects. It is likely that CAES using natural underground caverns could well face similar challenges.

Great progress has been made with electrical generation using wind power. The landscapes of many countries now bear witness to this. Wind turbines have the advantage of being able to generate day and night as long as the wind blows. The same issue of storage dogs this form of energy production, especially necessary when the demand is lower than the output or when the wind speeds are not high enough to turn the turbine blades. Provided wind generation shares the overall stage with other forms using more constant natural energy sources then wind can be successfully integrated with the existing countrywide power grids. As mentioned in the previous paragraph, tidal power falls into this category but is some way behind the advances made with wind generation. A more recent trend has been the placement of wind turbines offshore. This has a number of distinct advantages. The wind tends to be more constant in offshore environments compared with locations selected for development on land. These are invariably a compromise because of environmental considerations and public acceptability of such a development from the standpoint of visual and noise pollution. If the chosen site ends up being less than optimal as far as the constancy of generation is concerned, this has to be accepted. Offshore wind generation does have its own issues but it doesn't have to deal with topographical features affecting the wind direction, speed and constancy. The sites are less prone to public resistance, especially when they are more than 12 miles offshore and beyond the visual range from the adjacent land. Finally, there is effectively an inexhaustible supply of open space to locate the ideal number and size of turbines in a particular development which goes further to mitigate the cost differential between that and an onshore equivalent. This allows for optimisation as far as expensive underwater cabling is concerned and regular maintenance of the whole installation.

Transport has been under the spotlight for a number of years and is another area that governments have claimed boasting rights in order to demonstrate on-going success with their countries' conversion to renewable energy. To be more precise, it is only one section of transport, namely private cars. The advantages of tackling this section are quite significant. Firstly, a car requires fossil based fuel to power it which supports the continuation of exploring for, recovering and refining oil. Secondly, it contributes its own pollution and carbon dioxide emissions as it is operated. If a new pollution free process to power a car can be conceived, designed, tested, manufactured and then offered for sale to the car owning public then not only has a significant justification for the continuation of the extraction of fossil fuels been removed but so too has the consequential pollution caused by its operation. Rather cynically, governments have focussed on the private motorist because that is no more than a large group of their respective citizens who can be cajoled, enticed and ultimately threatened with breaking new laws if they do not renounce the use of their internal combustion engine (ICE) driven car and change to a more environmentally acceptable one. This is precisely what has happened in a number of countries around the world where laws have been passed which will forbid the sale of ICE powered cars by a certain date, and increasing time-based penalties introduced for those who elect to continue to drive them. Despite the pollution caused by private vehicles being relatively small when compared with electrical power generation, concentration on this sector is an effective way of encouraging people to be more thoughtful and reactive to the matter.

Of much greater concern are the other transportation sectors, namely shipping, road haulage, trains and aircraft most of which are either in the control of large companies, or the governments of sovereign states. None of these enterprises is as easily intimidated, especially when the solution is not obvious. All of them have a number of challenges in common. Whatever propulsion replaces the ICEs in road haulage, trains and shipping, it has to sustain the operation of the unit it is powering over long distances and for extended periods of time. A private car owner can be persuaded that 150-mile endurance is perfectly acceptable if the infrastructure is installed throughout the country to allow journeys of much greater distance to be tackled with occasional charging stops. A long haul commercial truck or lorry cannot operate within the same constraints. The electrical power units and associated batteries being designed and installed in private cars will require some dramatic advances in technology before they can be upscaled in terms of power output, endurance and weight to make them effective for such commercial service. It may be more practical in trains and in shipping as the weight burden can be accommodated more easily but endurance and power output remain a serious drawback.

As far as aircraft are concerned, while there have been some notable achievements announced and demonstrated with light aircraft using battery powered electric propulsion systems, once again these cannot be upscaled to power heavy jet transport aircraft even those carrying a modest number of passengers for a short distance. There are plans that are well advanced to work with liquid hydrogen and a modified version of the gas turbines that currently power aircraft while burning fossil fuels. However, much design and development will need to be undertaken before any prototype takes off. In addition, the infrastructure necessary to be put in place to support such a radical change will be another potential for delay. Hydrogen is most easily and cheaply produced from fossil fuel and is therefore, not deemed 'Green'. There are methods to produce it from other feedstock but the technology is either in its infancy or it will require dedicated large scale renewable electrical generation to support it. While there can be an almost limitless amount of effort and resource devoted to the development of such infrastructure, it is inevitable that it will lag the parallel processes required to prove the safety and effectiveness of the new generation of aircraft. This is for the simple reason that until the new design is proven, there will be an inevitable reluctance to commit to the levels of investment needed for the supporting infrastructure.

It is not difficult by concentrating on all the positive information being made available through media to reach the conclusion that a large part of the developed world has been making steady progress towards the goal of 'Zero Carbon' and is on track to meet the mid-century target. Sadly, it appears that is not the case. The discussion presented in the previous pages has concentrated on just two industry sectors, power generation and storage and on transportation. While both sectors have benefitted from being the subject of extensive media attention and independent government announcements, there has been no effort to map out and publish even an elementary programme of how either sector is approaching the problem of reaching Zero Carbon, even less how it proposes to achieve it. Many democratic governments in the developed world have made announcements concerning their latest record percentages of 'Renewable Energy' serving their respective grids but none has identified what these percentages mean in absolute terms simply because as welcome as these milestones are, they are merely scratching the surface of the problem and little else. To give just one example, there is a single power station in Europe[5] driven by the burning of a combination of locally mined and imported coal with a generation capacity measured in Gigawatt/hours, they are more usually in the Megawatt/hour range, and which is providing power to millions of homes and industry. This facility discharges more carbon dioxide into the atmosphere than the whole of the country of New Zealand and yet that State's Government has declared that there is no possibility of it being decommissioned and its output replaced by renewable energy until at least 2035 because it is so critical to the country's very survival.

The European Union has recently announced that it is addressing the problem of whether to declare natural gas and nuclear derived power as being 'Green'. A consensus on this needs to be achieved by a significant majority of the member Sovereign States before it can be formally declared an EU position. It is highly likely that such a decision will be hung, firstly because nuclear power is an extremely polarising subject, in no small part because its safety has been the subject of a media driven frenzy for the last 50 years, and secondly because natural gas is a fossil fuel which the less informed majority tells the world it should be banning. This non-decision will result in a significant percentage of the developed world being seen as either unable or unwilling to confront some of the real challenges and possible solutions to the Earth's current crisis. It is particularly sad that the EU will be hamstrung in taking any sort of lead in the nuclear debate, especially when one of its key member states has been satisfying the bulk of its country-wide electrical demand from Nuclear Power plants since the late 1950s, all without incident. The longer any such debate continues, the less likely it is that any of the solutions proposed to deal with the crisis will benefit from the consideration of nuclear power as an option. As for natural gas being seen as 'Green' when used as an energy source for electrical generation, it is only possible when it is considered in parallel with carbon capture and sequestration. Put simply, that means diverting all the atmospheric discharge from such a power station through a purpose designed and built treatment plant located adjacent to the power station, recovering the carbon and by various means, preventing it from reaching the atmosphere. This may be achieved by solidifying and burying it or pumping it as a gas into a permanent storage facility. There are already plants in operation around the world which have proven these technologies. However, they are expensive, technically challenging to build and operate, and ideally, require the location of the treatment plant to be close to subterranean geological features in which the captured carbon can be stored. If the use of fossil fuels is to remain integrated with the world's power generation and distribution in the future, then this can only be countenanced in concert with carbon capture and it is imperative that no reference should ever be made to their future use in a 'Green' society without it.

Most countries in the developed world use fossil fuels for power generation. Transforming this infrastructure to produce the same quantity of power with the same dependability but from 'renewable' energy sources is an enormous task. To date, there is not a single country that could produce a detailed transition schedule, and present it with any confidence of its acceptability, to an independent third party for scrutiny. It is simply too complex and involves a plethora of stakeholders, whose livelihoods and businesses would be directly or indirectly affected by the process. While the contracts to supply fossil fuel from the coal miners and the oil and gas companies around the world can be terminated, the consequences will be severe, in some cases denying an entire country a huge part of its income. This will have a knock-on effect with other industries that support the mining and oil and gas production and will eat into the very fabric of the country's society, seriously impacting its ability to provide education, healthcare and other basic services to its citizens. The country will also have to deal with widespread unemployment.

It is true that the transition to a 'Green' based economy will bring with it a multitude of new opportunities, new technologies and new wealth but not every country will be able to adapt easily or within the timeframes that are required. The societies that have developed and grown around the world have done so based on some very fundamental ingredients, the most significant being 'natural' resources. As the title suggests, these are naturally occurring resources such as minerals which are in plentiful supply, relatively easy to extract and are highly tradeable, either in their raw state or once refined, an energy source, an abundance of fresh water, a labour force, an equitable climate, a global location that allows inexpensive access to other countries and geographical features which enable seaports to be developed. Sometimes, not all of these 'ingredients' are present and so the development is slower. If the country has an aggressive determination to be successful, then it will rely on importing what it lacks. In the past this has included everything from energy in the form of liquid natural gas, oil or coal, labour for those countries who only have a small population but have a great wealth of other ingredients, or minerals such as iron ore, copper and bauxite. This international trading has not only established and sustained a country's economy but also it has become the very essence of the world economy. Now it seems that one of the fundamental building blocks or 'ingredients' of industrialised societies of the world has to be removed and replaced with an alternative. Other ingredients will hold their value but perhaps not in the same proportion as before. Where a country has been totally dependent on its oil and gas extraction and production, not only for its own energy requirements but because it has nothing else of value to trade with, then tomorrow's world will place it and its people in a desperate predicament. Somehow it must replace those resources with something else but even if that were possible it could take several generations to achieve.

So far, the discussion has centred on the 'Developed' world but what about those countries that are still developing? These are the countries that for political, geographic, climatic, sheer size of land mass or population have not come as far along the path prescribed by the Industrial Revolution. If they are to continue along that path as others have done before, then is it equitable and reasonable to expect them to redefine their development in such a way as to slow it down, make it much more expensive and perhaps less achievable, thereby delaying the delivery of basic facilities and services to their peoples that others already have? This would seem to be an inevitable outcome if they are to be denied the use of fossil fuels for future power generation or be asked to shut down those facilities that they have only recently commissioned and wait for more expensive and often, yet to be developed alternatives. The only way this scenario can be avoided is for the developed world to direct and share its attention and its resources in equal measure between its own requirements and those of its less well established neighbours. This is an imperative.

The other substantial grey area surrounds those countries that don't enjoy a liberal inclusive political environment but instead have a system of government that is authoritarian and autocratic. There are two in particular that fit such a category, China and Russia. The former is one of the largest emitters of carbon dioxide in the world, while Russia is in the top ten. Both countries have demonstrated an ability to silence their internal detractors by subversive means. Both have ongoing disputes with neighbouring countries which they consider should be under their control. Both use repeated shows of force against these target countries, presumably designed to intimidate and demonstrate their determination to 'right a wrong' as they see it. Both regimes are secretive and will deny the rest of the world access to information which other countries would share willingly. China is of particular concern as a result of its continued secretive behaviour over the origins of the Covid-19 pandemic. It is so assured of itself on the world stage that it sees no need to conform to the requests of internationally recognised and blatantly neutral institutions such as the World Health Organisation. Both have very substantial military capabilities. Based on these behaviours that have been witnessed over the last 50 years, is it reasonable for the rest of the world to expect that either of them will conform to the imperatives surrounding the need for massive change?

Of course, there are other countries who demonstrate similar behaviours as China and Russia. The fact that they are smaller does not diminish the implicit danger in their non-compliance but at least they are in the minority and there is always the possibility that engagement will be possible with some of them in the future.

From this brief look at some of the practicalities of translating the industries of the world from fossil fuel dependence to renewable alternatives, it is apparent that there are some very significant hurdles to be cleared. In themselves, these are not a justification to shy away from the issues. It may be that the associated societal upheaval and the anticipated international obfuscation present such an overwhelming challenge that living with the early effects of Climate Change becomes an inevitable outcome. But in the meantime, the inertia for change must be maintained on as many fronts as possible, not the least being with the person in the street.

Chapter Four
The Person in the Street

If the current predictions being shared on the media come to fruition, then the next 10 to 15 years could well see the end of the internal combustion engine as a power unit for the private motor car. Even if this doesn't eventuate right across the globe, it is likely that the days will be numbered for any remaining ICEs in their current form. This means that hundreds of millions of humans will have played a very direct role in mitigation measures being aimed at containing the adverse effects of climate change. The fact that this response is being forced upon some of them by state governments in concert with manufacturers has already been suggested. However, the legislation is still some way off coming into effect and so it is heartening to see many people taking the initiative earlier rather than leaving it to the last minute. Of course, private cars are driven by a very large cross-section of the communities of the world. They are not confined to one particular group, although a certain level of wealth is a prerequisite. Many purchasers of the new electrically propelled vehicles could be motivated by the fear of their cars that they are replacing being rendered valueless if they leave the changeover too close to the legislation coming into effect. Some will have made the decision from a point of genuine concern and a desire to make some positive contribution to the challenges that lie ahead. The people in this group are especially important to the collective worldwide response because there is a great deal that humanity can achieve at an individual level. However, it requires knowledge, a willingness to reflect on the issues that are being faced and admit to the potential personal contribution that each member of society has made, and finally to possess or at least begin to develop an intense empathy with the environment in its broadest context.

In the earlier chapters, some of the benefits that have accrued to individual members of society throughout the Industrial Revolution have been identified.

The early days were quite brutal with many more people suffering compared with those that benefitted. But slowly this situation changed, and fewer people were exploited while more and more enjoyed the fruits of the Revolution. Today, millions upon millions of human souls all over the world can enjoy a standard of living undreamt of at the outset but all at a heavy price. Each watt of electrical power that is used, each glass of fresh drinking water that is consumed, each flush of the toilet that is made, each material possession that is acquired, each journey that is conducted by private car, train, aircraft or ship, every item of food that is purchased and prepared for consumption, each item of clothing that is acquired, each use of the motorised lawn mower, hedge trimmer, log splitter or other labour saving household device, each theatre or cinema visit, each visit to a hospital or other support facility all result in or have already resulted in the release of carbon into the atmosphere. Yes, the manufacturers, the facility operators, the businesses are nearly always the prime polluters but if society was to reflect more intensely on the necessity of what is purchased, consumed or undertaken, then this would have an enormous impact on the speed with which the planet is being polluted. It will not reverse the massive levels of pollution already released but it will reduce the daily discharges from now on, and if it comes with that greater reflection on how lives are conducted in the future then it could well play a part in the very dramatic but necessary readjustment that will help to save the planet and prevent it from veering too far away from the conditions that are enjoyed today.

This is a huge undertaking. It dwarfs that which is expected of industry and governments. What is being suggested is the elevation of humankind to the next level, one at which each human has discovered its innate ability, sensitivity, willingness and conscious awareness to see each interaction with another or with the environment, for what it is and not just as the story that each has told itself. But before this tectonic shift can be investigated further, it is important to understand more of the practical issues that lie behind the current predicament.

When humans began making things for themselves which would improve, either their or the lives of others, it marked a significant inflection point in societal development. Instead of focussing on the simple matter of survival, having shelter in the form of a house, food to eat, clothing and warmth and a means to provide all this, gradually another imperative emerged. This was the acquisition of material wealth. This had already been a feature of the more privileged members of society for some time, mostly those whose birthright or hard work had positioned them above others in terms of wealth. They were the landowners, the farmers, the mill owners, the elite of what was essentially an agricultural-based society. Their wealth came from what they were able to grow and sell using country labour or how much wheat and corn they could mill and sell to bakers and brewers. The manifestation of their material wealth was seen through the clothes that they wore, the horses, carriages and houses that they owned, and in the furniture and fittings that adorned them. But as manufacturing took hold and there was an alternative to farm work, so there was a steady flow of people from the countryside to the bigger towns and cities where industry was establishing itself. There, work could be found in the new factories making all manner of things such as household items, fasteners, tools and glass, in the mines recovering tin, copper, iron ore and coal and in the burgeoning textile industry weaving and manufacturing garments. Much of the output would be sold overseas while the remainder would begin to find its way into local homes. Within the space of a few generations, the landscape had changed completely. People were beginning to appreciate what could be owned that would make their lives more comfortable whether it was a steel coal scuttle to keep coal ready to burn and shaped to throw lumps of it onto a fire without spilling them in the grate or a mechanical device made to wring clothes out to speed up drying after they had been washed or the replacement of the candle in the dish with an oil lamp burning whale oil, they all helped with the trials of living and became material possessions that people hankered after. The variety of items was enormous. Of course, the take up was slow, very varied from region to region and less obvious at its outset. But it grew right through the nineteenth and on into the twentieth century. Gradually, manufacture spread beyond country limits and new centres emerged overseas. These nearly always benefitted from much cheaper labour. Initially, overseas manufactured items were scorned, unless they were made by a recognised specialist producer such as optics made in Germany. Otherwise, products lacked the quality that the home produced ones were seen to have and there was a measure of elitism evident in the origin of which one was owned. This has never really been extinguished and today's marketing and sales initiatives rely heavily on it to entice the buyer to purchase the more expensive product.

As the cost of labour grew in developed countries, so the manufacture of products in still developing countries became more and more attractive. Cheaper products, provided that the quality could be maintained, would ensure a bigger slice of the overall market. This would mean more sales, more revenue, more profit and more wealth for the business owners and all their stakeholders. By the third quarter of the twentieth century, the volume and diversity of manufactured goods produced overseas, which were available to purchase in the developed countries, was dramatically different from earlier in the century. Of course, there were two World Wars which upset the overall growth of not only manufacturing but also the provision of utilities. Ironically the Second World War had the reverse effect on some nations. But if the growth is demonstrated graphically from its outset at the very end of the 17th century to today, then these two events would be seen as little more than blips on an otherwise steady upward curve. Since the end of the Second World War, the curve's slope has become significantly steeper.

As the world navigated the end of the millennium amid global fears of an information technology crisis, based on the idea that millions of computer-controlled services which influenced, impacted or directly affected the lives of most of the world's citizens, might well crash at midnight, simply because of perceived programming anomalies to do with date recognition, material based capitalism was flourishing as never before. The information anxiety came to nought and life moved on into the twenty-first century. Not only were the democracies of the world revelling in their material wealth but so too were some of the more autocratic and authoritarian regimes because they had become the suppliers, the workshops to the world. In a balanced and possibly utopian world where the objectives of the leaders of all of the Sovereign States are broadly in alignment and recourse to conflict, regardless of the situation, is never entertained as a solution to anything, then the idea of concentrating the manufacture of goods or the provision of different services, which the whole world needs, in places which can provide them most efficiently and inexpensively seems to be a very sound concept. A parallel model must surely be a large business corporation which is looking to expand itself and acquire other complementary businesses. As it does this, there is likely to be some overlap, where the acquired company, as a part of its business portfolio makes similar products or offers similar services as the acquiring company. It is a logical and progressive step to evaluate which entity makes the product or provides the services more cheaply and more efficiently. Unless there are other less obvious considerations to take account of, it is then a simple matter of closing down one operation and concentrating all the efforts for the provision of that particular service or manufacturing process on the chosen one. There are countless examples of this in the business world, and if the analysis has been carried out correctly and the redundant human and equipment resources have been redeployed effectively elsewhere, then the future is invariably a bright one for all concerned. But this is a parallel model from the business world, not the world comprising sovereign states. Businesses are not countries even if some of them have gross turnovers nearing or exceeding the Gross Domestic Product (GDP) of entire nations. The management and leadership of a large corporation are, by definition autocratic and invariably less than democratic even though it may operate from a Western Democratic country. Theoretically, this allows a corporation to behave in any way it wishes provided that it remains within the laws of the country in which it is based. In reality, it has to behave itself if it is to survive because there are all sorts of more subtle controllers that affect its success and profitability. It has to trade with other businesses. It has to provide its customers with cost effective and serviceable products. It must pay attention to the welfare of its workforce and avoid high levels of staff turnover. It must be seen to be a good corporate citizen, or it will begin to lose its standing in the marketplace hierarchy. It can be seen from this brief explanation that the behaviours of corporations and large businesses that make up the heart of Western Democracy's capitalist society, are effectively regulated by the environment in which they operate. If they ignore this regulation, then their ultimate success will be severely compromised, and usually, in a relatively short timeframe. That compromise will be seen in staff disaffection and consequential high turnover, in difficult communications with customers and other businesses, in the loss of business and market position, and eventually, in turnover and profit. This will impact its share value and if the matters that have caused this are not checked, lead to the ultimate demise of the business. Although simplistic in its presentation, the outcomes described are inevitable and well understood. Of course, this doesn't stop corporations sailing very close to the wind and running successful and profitable businesses while they are acknowledged as being both corrosive and bullying within their structures. However, that is another subject.

When it comes to comparing corporations with sovereign states in terms of the effective division of responsibility for the international supply of commonly required products or services, the biggest difference lies in their regulation. Assuming that the country in question is not a democracy but rather, one run by an autocratic regime then the issues will compound very quickly. Superficially, the requirement to provide quality products and services in a competitive, cost effective and timely manner should be enough of an incentive for the country to perform to the highest standards. Being in this position enables it to provide employment for its citizens, which in turn enables them to house and feed themselves. It provides funds to the state not only through business and income tax but also through import and export duties. On the world stage, the country can claim boasting rights for the efficient and competitive supply of products and services to the rest of the world. Of course, there is one glaring issue with the whole arrangement. It has been established on the back of a seemingly inexhaustible supply of cheap labour when compared with the remainder of the world. This was one of the founding reasons for its success on the world stage. It is probable that this labour force would have no way of affording any of the products that it is helping to produce. They are all destined for the Western world. Many would have no idea what they are manufacturing because the society they live in is very different. Were it not for the level of worldwide communication that is enjoyed, there would be little risk of them ever finding out what life was like in the West. The state authorities are wise to this and so the volume and content of information about western life finding its way into their country is rigorously controlled. Despite this, there is a very real risk that the workforce will slowly come to understand what they are making and what it is being used for. If that is coupled with a growing awareness of what freedoms, facilities, resources, services and luxuries the West enjoys, it is quite likely that the state will have an increasingly disgruntled workforce on its hands. In the near term, this is likely to be controlled in the way insurgencies are handled in such states, by coercion and force. How long the lid can be kept on this particular boiling pot will remain to be seen. Of course, if there was open international dialogue, there would be the prospect of the matter being discussed between state leaders on a global scale, help could be sought and a solution to the problem teased out. Instead, the western democratic customers can only sit back and watch.

The depth and extent of this phenomenon is now alarming. Put quite simply, the West has now substantially lost its ability to make things. It has been an insidious process which has occurred progressively over the last two or three decades but it has been shown to be very far reaching to the point that during the recent pandemic, the world was largely dependent on one country alone to produce the Personal Protective Equipment (PPE) that has been needed so desperately to control the spread of the Coronavirus. There are still pockets of production about the West, particularly for specialist equipment, tools, luxury goods, pharmaceuticals and weapons but the vast bulk of all manufacturing including nuts and bolts, PPE, clothes, shoes, kitchen utensils, batteries, white goods, motor cars and trucks to name but a few have all been assigned elsewhere. The manufactured price, quality, volume, and shipping are all so attractive that the distributors, wholesalers and retailers of the West simply cannot entertain seeking out an alternative supply. Meanwhile, the skills of the western workforces have been in steady decline, the manufacturing facilities have been demolished or re-purposed and the economies have been realigned to balance the individual country's books by other means. So not only does the world have a problem with its levels of manufacturing, its profligate use of precious raw materials and the consequential pollution of the planet, but it has also allowed the responsibility for that production to reside in countries that have questionable moral and ethical values such that dialogue at anything other than a perfunctory level is hard if not impossible.

It is against this world political backdrop, that the person in the street is being asked to make a difference. The media, governments, action groups and other supposedly concerned citizens have all tended to point the finger of blame be it at the oil and gas exploration and production companies, the coal mining industry, the power generation companies, the car manufacturers, the shipping companies, the airlines, the chemical and fertiliser producers, the transport companies, the list goes on. These are the polluters who are responsible for the world's predicament and so they must fix it. But as has been shown, these may well be the instruments of pollution but they are simply responding to an apparently insatiable worldwide demand. For them to cease their operation overnight would result in chaos. They are all inextricably woven into the fabric of the world society. That world society is simply responding to the very demands that it and its citizens make on it. Bits of it might be fixed by legislation and some evidence of that has been seen with the eventual outlawing of the ICE in private vehicles by some democratic governments. That might prove to be quite a useful catalyst which will help to stimulate other actions but it will not work in isolation and might even end up being less than helpful. As counter intuitive as it sounds, it is the person in the street who bears the responsibility for what has happened and it is that person who possesses the greatest power to effect change but that power has to be acknowledged, understood, and then put into action.

It's quite possible that they can be given a substantial hand with their task by the very governments and industries that are either gently coercing them by legislation or who are wrapping and marketing the new vehicles and associated systems for their consumption. There are two distinct ways that this can be achieved. The first is to draw attention to a number of hard engineering facts. Vehicles powered by an electric drive train are dramatically more efficient than those powered by an ICE[1,2]. This simply compares the electrical energy transferred to the wheels of the car all the way from a coal fired power station where it was generated, with the petrol derived energy produced by drilling for oil, recovering it, and refining it for use in a car. The pollution coming from the extraction of raw materials and the manufacture of the batteries that store the energy in the car is, in many cases, higher than that released when building an ICE. However, once the two vehicles are running side by side on the road, the electrically driven has virtually no harmful emissions whereas the ICE will continue to pollute the atmosphere for the rest of its running life. These adverse manufacturing figures are based largely on information from China, the world's largest automobile battery manufacturer[3]. It is envisaged that future technology will reduce the battery manufacturing pollution dramatically. There are other technical advantages to electric power trains which make huge engineering sense when compared with the ICE. When these are added to the pollution reduction and raw material requirements, the argument for their adoption becomes overwhelming. It is the responsibility of governments, manufacturers, distributors and retail sales outlets to package these benefits and present them as simply and objectively as possible. Here, then is one of the original drivers behind the Industrial Revolution being harnessed once again for the good of humankind.

The second is to draw specific attention to the positive outcomes as far as the environment is concerned and to relate those to each and every purchaser and user of an electric powered vehicle. This is not a case of bombarding people with endless rows of facts and figures but rather to learn to speak in more spiritual tones. Humankind is a part of the environment. The understanding and appreciation of that concept has been ignored, refuted and trampled on. It is time to establish the reconnection.

Chapter Five
Is Humanity Really Aware of
Its Own Footprint?

As has already been intimated, the planet Earth is extraordinarily old when measured by any human scale, about four and a half billion years. It has evolved steadily over its life, metamorphosing repeatedly until it arrived at the state that is recognised today. The middle of Earth has remained molten but a thick cool crust formed on the outside and this usually keeps everything relatively stable. Sometimes some of the middle finds its way through the crust where it is a bit weaker, or where one section of it slides over or under another piece. This can result in an earthquake or sometimes in the explosive formation of a volcano, often seen and recognised as a conical mountain with a crater at the summit instead of the point of the cone. Molten material, gas and entrained solids created the original shape and whenever there is a new eruption, these are all ejected into the atmosphere. Depending on the ferocity of the eruption, this material can be launched high into the Earth's atmosphere and remain there for some time. As the Earth cooled, this was quite a frequent occurrence but over time, things calmed down. Today, there are lots of volcanoes still dotting the Earth's surface but they tend to erupt less frequently. Many of them are regarded as being extinct and appear to have no further active life left in or under them. Occasionally, a new volcano is formed but this is no longer the common experience it was several billion years ago.

These violent events, especially when witnessed 'in the flesh' would have been indescribably traumatic and assuming the witnesses survived they would have had a profound and lasting effect on them. They offered a visual, audible, and olfactory image of the enormous power associated with the natural events that occurred during the formation of the planet. It is difficult to appreciate the size and violence of the explosion that formed Lake Taupo, New Zealand's largest lake some 27,000 years ago. It is a super volcano that began its life 263,000 years before that. The lake now fills the caldera or collapsed crater. Humanity didn't reach New Zealand until about 500 years after the last notable eruption which was 1800 years ago. The countryside around the lake is now populated but relatively modestly compared with the lower slopes of Mount Vesuvius in Italy where there are well over 600,000 souls who live within that volcano's prescribed danger zone. It has already demonstrated its destructive power less than 2,000 years ago and the stark evidence of how it affected the lives of those living adjacent to it at the time can still be seen in the remains of Pompei and Herculaneum, the two Roman settlements that bore the brunt of it. Roman eyewitness accounts written soon afterwards can be read if additional evidence of the enormity of the eruption is needed[1]. And yet, the population to the North West of the volcano, south of the city of Naples seems to remain largely indifferent to its threat.

Could it be that the existence of volcanic activity around the globe has somehow inured human beings to the existential danger it poses, and could that indifference be passed on to include the less obvious atmospheric pollution that is also a significant consequence? If that was the case, then was the London smog[2] of the 1950s and the possible long term consequences of it just passed off in people's minds as being no worse than any other sort of naturally occurring polluting event? They were the result of the combination of damp weather, soot particles from burning coal and other gases released from both domestic and industrial fires all combining to create an appallingly toxic environment throughout the greater part of London. Although the defining event was in 1952, it became a regular occurrence during successive winters resulting in both severe respiratory illness and death. The matter was addressed over time and the smogs became less frequent but there would be consequences projected long into the future. The volcanic eruptions that had been seen on cinema news reels or had been read about in books must have left some sort of impression. Was the connection ever made between what was happening on the Earth's surface and what the long term effects might be, or were people just too busy living day to day, making ends meet, recovering after the cruel years of the Second World War and trying to build a better life for themselves and their children?

There was other less glamorous evidence of environmental abuse closer to the homes of those who would never experience a volcanic eruption or earthquake. Violent storms have always been a regular occurrence in nearly every part of the globe. They would often leave huge swathes of destruction in their paths, uprooted trees, flattened crops, flooded fields and landslides. If the results of storms impacted the lives of people living locally then efforts would be made to repair the damage and reinstate roads, bridges and any other damage to infrastructure. Was there any consideration given to the damage to the natural environment caused by the enormous amount of silt that was spread over the countryside as a result of the flooding? This would have destroyed plant life and maybe, whole ecosystems. Or was the view that it was a natural event and therefore, nature would take care of it? Perhaps there was a 'Eureka moment' when film began emerging of the testing of nuclear weapons which happened for an alarming length of time after the war. Maybe the more fundamental issue of the overall potential damage to the environment was overshadowed by the health fear associated with the release of radioactive material. There was certainly a very vocal response to atmospheric testing and eventually it was halted. However, tests of various intensities have continued underground.

At a much more mundane level, the perpetual scattering of waste across the countryside is a clear example of humanity's indifference to pollution. This is usually a waste that people could have taken responsibility for and carried with them until an appropriate place was found to throw it away. Many of today's industrial areas which occupy the margins of towns and cities are instantly identifiable by the mass of manufacturing waste simply discarded about the periphery of each site. In areas of the world that have not yet devised and put into practice an effective and nationwide refuse recovery and treatment system, this is to be expected. Sadly, it remains the hallmark of a developing nation and can leave a lasting impression on the visitor. The cleanliness of a modern city speaks volumes to the sensitivity of its inhabitants.

Returning now to the Earth's crust, this is a quite remarkable feature of the planet. To begin with, it kept all the molten material well away from the surface. It provided a stable platform on which an environment or ecosystem of living things could develop and thrive, and it captured and stored both fresh and salt water which supported the environment. It also became the most wonderful repository for all sorts of material and resources which could be used in a multiplicity of ways once it was understood that they were there, what they were and how they might be used. This didn't happen until very approximately, 50,000 years ago. That was when a particular animal species that had only very recently formed a part of the ecosystem, began to be more adventurous with its surroundings. This was quite an extraordinary turn of events because there had been other species living on the earth for as much as 30 million years at a stretch and yet they hadn't seemed to advance at all. The 'adventurous one' was, of course, 'Homo sapiens'. It developed at an extraordinary rate when compared with any other sentient beings. There were many reasons for this, some of them quite logical and understandable, others less so. Regardless, this species advanced quickly learning to live together in small communities, care for one another, make maximum use of its surroundings and eventually stamp its own ideas on this very environment of which it was a part.

It would be difficult to comment with any authority on the relationship early Homo sapiens enjoyed with its surrounding ecosystem. History suggests that if there was a spiritual connection where it was appreciated and understood that a balance did exist within the ecosystem between all of its component parts, of which homo sapiens was just one, then it was lost and any substantive evidence suggesting that this symbiosis might have been understood by homo sapiens was subsumed by the practical necessities of using the system for its own ends. Many theories have been postulated, argued over and peer reviewed as to whether it existed and was lost, whether it never existed or whether it was always there and remains in some very small percentage of Earth dwelling humans today. Some of these theories have ended up in mainstream evolutionary history as being 'The most probable'. Where religion appears in these debates, it seems to neither add to nor detract from the various theories. Whatever passage the relationship took, ultimately it morphed into a feeling of superiority that nature and the glorious environment that enveloped the globe, had evolved principally for the enjoyment and exclusive benefit of humankind. Until quite recently when some governments have been coerced by a vocal minority to set some limits on what should and shouldn't be perpetrated on the environment in the name of development, humankind has been content to commit the most appalling atrocities. It has thought nothing of clearing vast tracts of woodland for the purpose of building ships. It has mined for enormous volumes of the precious ingredients found near the surface of the earth's crust and has piled the tailings over wide areas irrevocably altering the local environment. It has flooded huge valleys for the purpose of storing water to drink or to power turbines to make electricity. It has dammed rivers to control the natural flow of water in order to redistribute it downstream for commercial gain. In the process, the delicate river ecosystems have been disturbed, habitats for other animals have been destroyed, and in some cases, entire species of animal have been wiped out. Vast areas of natural woodland have been cleared to make way for farms to supply the ever-increasing demands of humanity. Wetlands have been drained for the same purpose, destroying yet more natural habitats. Acre upon acre of concrete and bitumen has been poured or laid all over the Earth's surface to house people, provide infrastructural support, industrial development and communication. Offshore, huge fishing fleets have scoured the oceans for fish with little or no regard for the future. Whole species have been fished almost to extinction. If the boats are not hauling their huge catches on board to provide food, then they are fishing selectively for the purpose of sport. This behaviour has been mirrored on land with humankind's appetite for hunting which has seen the drastic and potentially irreversible reduction of wild animals deemed worthy of being shot as trophies or worse for their potential as suppliers of exotic elixirs, both of which sustain highly profitable businesses.

While all this very visible desecration and destruction has been going on in the name of commerce and world development, the waste products of industrialisation have been seeping and creeping back into the very environment that has already been subject to repeated rape and pillage. Rivers and coastlines have been polluted with sewage, nitrogen saturated water run-off from farming, innumerable cocktails of chemicals from industrial plants and highly concentrated saline solution from onshore desalination plants to name but a few of the sources and their poisons. Then there is the solid waste, the plastic bags, the fishing nets, the detritus of daily living which all finds its way into the waterways and oceans of the world. And last but by no means the least, the gaseous pollution which is now at the very heart of the future viability of humanity. Of course, it is more insidious than any other pollutant because it is difficult to see. The media loves to portray it as steam rising from the cooling towers of the world's industries. This may be a symbolic gesture but it certainly isn't carbon dioxide or methane, nor is it particularly representative of the types of industry that cause the worst pollution. So have cooling towers belching steam become the international symbol for Climate Change? If they have, then they have arrived there at best as a result of ignorance and at worst through a desire to point the finger of blame at industry as a whole. Now the media is supposed to represent the citizens of the world, seek out truth for them, and reflect what the majority is thinking or worrying about and act as a collective voice. If this is the case, then they too have slipped comfortably into the blame culture. To some, it appears that the media throughout the world has become progressively more anti-establishment, particularly over the last 50 years. It is now difficult to find examples of objective reporting and editorial writing, perhaps because it no longer sells copy as in days of yore. It seems much more effective to climb on the bandwagon of disaffection and let rip at whatever is vogue at the time. Indeed, it is hard to see what side the Fourth Estate is now supporting besides its own.

Changes in the conventions of society don't happen overnight unless there is some cataclysmic event that makes it impossible to continue in the same way. While the spectre of Climate Change carries with it the prospect of increased global temperatures, rises in sea level, a destabilisation of the world's climate characteristics that have come to be recognisable and understood, and probably many other environmental changes that are not fully appreciated at this stage, the process will be a gradual one, developing over a number of years. By the time the changes are visible or can be felt, it will of course be too late. And so, if there is to be action to mitigate these projected issues then it must begin now and it must be based on trust rather than visible and incontrovertible evidence. It is this question of trust which is causing anxiety in some, indifference in others and outright rejection in the remainder.

If the spectre of Climate Change is to be faced and dealt with by humanity, then there are certain things which must happen quickly. There are a million and one practical issues that can be tackled and as has been shown, many are underway already. However, on their own they represent little more than a fleet of ambulances at the bottom of the cliff. They might ameliorate the worst of the predicted outcomes if they can be implemented right across the globe in time but unless humanity changes its behaviour, these practical tinkerings will turn out to be little more than a temporary fix which will be overwhelmed by the next cycle of abusive treatment measured out to the natural environment. In order to tackle the malaise effectively, it is imperative that humankind is taught to understand its place in the natural world, to accept the necessity of maintaining an appropriate balance between all the components of it, of which humanity is a critical one, and putting these teachings into effect as soon as is humanly possible.

So what is to be taught? Is it just a case of imploring the world not to throw their empty boxes of McDonald's out of the car window, not to discard their sump oil at the boundary of their property when they have just completed an oil change on their car, not to pour old cooking oil and other fats into the kitchen sink, not to leave their broken washing machines and other household electrical goods on the nearest piece of empty ground for someone else to collect and take to a recognised disposal site, not to ride their trail bikes, motorised or pedal powered, in areas of parkland where it is expressly forbidden, or is there something much more fundamental and sensitive to be addressed? There is no doubt that each and every human being on the planet can play its part in cleaning up its immediate environment and disciplining itself and its charges to keep it that way in the future. There are countless examples of unfriendly actions towards the environment that must be dealt with in this way. But these are really just the tip of an iceberg. The bulk of the changes are buried deep in the core of the ice and require much more introspection and thought to even understand, let alone address. The Industrial Revolution has been so successful that millions upon millions of human beings have found themselves feeling entitled and deserving of all the labour-saving devices money can buy. One of the greatest of these items has been the private car. Of course, it is human energy saving, it is a great vehicle for communication; it has opened up all sorts of work opportunities not only for those who are a part of their manufacture but also for those who use them. It has reduced the sense of isolation experienced by outlying communities and brought the simple joy of travel to so many. The impact of the private car on Climate Change has already been discussed in terms of the pollution inherent in its manufacture and use, but what might the consequences have been for the owners? All animals, all sentient beings require exercise in order to maintain their physical condition. The less exercise human beings take, the less fit they become and the more prone to weight gain. The more weight they put on, the more their bodily health is challenged and the less inclined they become to take exercise. It is a simple connection made almost infinitely complex by the amount of discussion, research, reflection and opinion focussed on it. So the question this direction of thought demands is what negative impact has something like the private car or vehicle had on humankind? If it has resulted in less exercise being taken initially in the form of walking and later cycling, because it is easier, more comfortable and quicker to travel by car then has that choice contributed even in a modest way to the degradation of the health of the populations of the developed world? For anyone living adjacent to a busy road, especially one that doesn't have a pavement or footpath designated for walkers and possibly, cyclists, then the prospect of sharing the roadway with private cars, commercial vehicles and heavy goods trucks or lorries is not only almost overwhelming but also potentially extremely dangerous. Of course, it is done daily by a hardy cross-section of any community, by those who are inured to the inherent dangers and simply enjoy the exercise or others who don't have access to a vehicle but have a basic need to travel. The resulting accidents and deaths are a regular news feature. Over the last 30 years, there has been a progressive move to design and build facilities to accommodate cyclists, especially in the larger towns and cities but it has been a slow process, and in many countries, it remains the exception rather than the rule. As for walking, especially along country routes, this seems as if it is no longer a recognised means of travel. If humanity has suffered in this manner, then that suffering has put more strain on the health services, which has resulted in the increase in the use of dedicated energy to run the health services' facilities which has increased the need for more electricity to be generated, which has added to the pollution of the planet. In short, the provision of a facility to make life easier and more enjoyable has brought with it an unintentional consequence, maybe even more damaging to society than Climate Change.

If the cause and effect described above is not acknowledged, it is perhaps not surprising. It is quite a severe indictment and some of the linkages might be regarded as somewhat tenuous. However, this is the type and level of connectivity that needs to be made across a wide range of human activity if the appropriate level of ownership of the problem is to be made. Taking exercise is very much more popular than it used to be 40 or 50 years ago. Health experts throughout the world have been extolling the virtues of doing so for a similar time period. Today, the manufacturers and retailers of the world's market economy have jumped onto the bandwagon to provide clothes and equipment for taking exercise. The entrepreneurs of nearly every society have seen the business potential and profit associated with gyms and fitness centres and a certain section and age group of each has responded. This is heartening but does it reflect a genuine acknowledgment of what is required 'across the board' or is it simply the latest fashion or fad to grip the market economies of the world? It should not be forgotten that one of the prime motivations for taking exercise is the simple enjoyment of it but do those who participate in exercise realise the deeper significance of what they are doing, of how they are being responsible for themselves, their bodies, their minds and most importantly, their environment? If they don't, how can they be helped to make the mental leap to the next level so that they can appreciate it and draw still more from it?

There are many loose ends left lying in the last few chapters that need to be brought together. Climate Change has been caused mainly by industrial pollution. Industry provides life sustaining goods and services to the population of the world. Industry has grown to the size and complexity that it has because of demand for its services and its products. That demand is self-perpetuating as it draws on a fundamental human trait that is always seeking to at least sustain and ideally improve its living conditions. Human beings are a part of the environment. Individually, they have knowingly damaged and abused it. The sense of intrinsic connection appears to have been lost in most developed societies. It has often been replaced by a sense of ownership. This could still be a form of connection but it is misplaced unless there is an intense understanding that goes hand in glove with it. There is no universal agreement on how to tackle Climate Change despite repeated meetings throughout the world. There is much tokenism evidenced by the response of individual sovereign states. There is a pressing need for a world climate change initiative but there is too much division in the world today to allow it to happen especially between China, Russia and the Western world. The balance of power in terms of manufacturing has been hugely distorted by the position the rest of the world has allowed and even encouraged China to assume. Those solutions that are offered to deal with a small fraction of the multiplicity of problems being faced by the world are invariably 'Overamped' by governments and media to suit differing agendas. This is both misleading and disingenuous. The person in the street has to come to terms with the damage that each one of them is doing every day and learn to reduce it. The world will not implode or be impossible to live on if nothing is done but living conditions will deteriorate for tens or even hundreds of millions and it is more than likely that this deterioration will lead to unrest or maybe worse. Is it this scenario that could lead to the realisation of a dystopian future to which humanity has been so pervasively attracted to in both literature and film?

Whatever the dynamics are today, now the pictures of Climate Change and the associated Global Warming have been presented to the world at large, it is no longer possible to withdraw those images. Attention will be fixated on the issues until all the implied threats have been addressed and dealt with to universal satisfaction or the pictures have simply become an accepted reality. Just as the picture of nuclear war became the dominant consequence of nuclear fission, so the prospect of utilising the glorious release of energy for peaceful and life enhancing purposes has been rendered almost impossible. The only circumstances that might derail the significance of the necessity of action against Climate Change would be a major global catastrophe of a proportion that would decimate the peoples of the world. Ironically, that could derive from nuclear war waged initially by those regimes who have demonstrated a blatant disregard for honesty, impartiality, respect and empathy with their own populations, the very ones which have already demonstrated their indifference towards dealing with Climate Change and yet remain some of the biggest releasers of carbon.

Chapter Six
Was Humanity Ever Enlightened?

The idea of a symbiotic relationship between Homo sapiens and the environment has already been raised. It is highly improbable that this didn't exist in some form between early humans and their environment. It would be difficult to contemplate any sort of long-term survival which excluded some measure of intimacy. What is rather more difficult to determine is at what level it existed. Animism is an acknowledged phase of human psychological development which is still evident in less developed societies today. In simple terms, this is a relationship that has been established between a human and an object, either animate or inanimate such that the human has attributed godlike qualities to the object in question. This could be something as simple as a fruit producing plant or tree, a large piece of rock or even a wild animal. This is not to be confused with the later stage of development which is sometimes referred to as the 'Mythic' level[1]. Here there is a community appreciation of a story or series of myths which may well be fantastic in their reach and improbability but nonetheless, helped people towards some sort of common understanding or vision within their community as to how the world about them has come to pass and what holds it together. Animism manifested itself earlier. It suggested a mind sufficiently unrestrained in terms of imagination to create pictures and stories other than those that were physically unfolding in front of it. It is likely that this was a part of an effort to try to give an explanation for the extraordinary natural process of fruit or nut production from a tree or bush. Where the Animistic object was an animal, then this could arise from a means of dealing with fear. If that fear could be given some sort of supernatural reality in the mind of the beholder by giving it a godlike identity within its environment, it might have offered some measure of comfort.

Animism was also looking for results. By elevating a producing plant or tree to a superhuman state, this would have demonstrated an appreciation of its superiority, thus encouraging it to continue to perform bountifully. Likewise, the animal that had been elevated in the same way might be less likely to attack its loyal and appreciative subjects as it was them who held it in high esteem. Regardless of the detail surrounding the origins of Animism, it is mentioned here merely to indicated that early humans did possess a fertile imagination and were in the habit of constructing stories to explain their environment. Whether this trait can be linked directly to a deeper understanding or sense of their environment is not so clear but it does suggest that humans had the mental ability to consider how a situation might look from another's perspective be it an animal, plant or inanimate object. On its own and without any more tangible anthropological evidence to back it up, it is also possible that such a conclusion could be misplaced.

The other picture that historical evidence paints is far more depressing. Homo sapiens is thought to have made the journey from the Euro/Asian land mass to Australasia via the multitude of islands that now make up Indonesia about 45,000 years ago. It would have required an extraordinarily courageous series of land and sea excursions to make the crossing. On arrival, the landscape, climate, flora and fauna would all have been very different from that which the explorers had left behind. Despite this, the invasion was successful and led to the permanent establishment of a very substantial number of communities across Australia that remained undisturbed for most of that 45,000 years. However, the cost to the natural environment was colossal. At the outset, Australia was home to the most fantastic array of wild animals, particularly mega fauna, many of them harmless to humans. There were the 200kg kangaroos that stood over two metres tall, the marsupial lion, similar in size to the Bengal tiger, flightless birds, twice the size of an ostrich, massive lizards, enormous koalas, the giant diprotodon, the wombat that grew to over 2,500 kgs and many others. Within the space of a few thousand years, all but one of these 24 species had been completely wiped out. They had become extinct. There are those that would blame a corresponding period of climate change as the responsible agent but there is no evidence to support these types of animals being sensitive to similar events in earlier or later times. It is very difficult, if not impossible to exonerate humanity from this atrocity. To compound matters, the invaders brought the deliberate and targeted use of fire with them. It was highly effective to clear areas of vegetation, driving out animals that could then be slaughtered thus adding further terror and despair to these original inhabitants. Although fire has existed as a natural chemical reaction, effectively since the planet's inception, its deliberate and controlled use became the exclusive domain of humanity. There seems to be little doubt that its widespread use throughout Australasia also resulted in a dramatic change in the flora, wiping out many of the original native tree species. There is little fossilised evidence of the existence of the prolific Eucalypt before the invasion. Once fire had become a common occurrence, this left the Eucalypt as the most prolific species to survive and thrive.

A similar picture occurred when the Asian based Homo sapiens moved across the gap between its eastern most flank and what is now Alaska about 14,000 years ago. Slowly and predictably, the invaders moved from their arrival point all the way down to the very bottom of South America, Tiera Del Fuego. It took several thousand years but it resulted in a similar desolation of animal species as had been seen some 30,000 years before in Australia. There were very few places on the planet that didn't succumb to humanity's wholesale thuggery against the animal kingdom. The islands of the Pacific met with the same fate, although New Zealand's glorious environment survived largely unadulterated until about 1200 years ago. One of the very few to survive were the Galapagos Islands where the giant tortoise still roams. Only by the most rigorous intervention championed initially by the naturalist Charles Darwin has it remained one of the most unspoilt places on earth as far as mega fauna is concerned.

There is certainly no animal species that has delivered so much wanton destruction to the environment and in such an incredibly short space of cosmic time. While there can be some measure of justification in terms of hunting for the sake of providing a food source, and because Homo sapiens, with its enormous brain power and use of handmade weapons had elevated itself to the top of the food chain, at least on land, it still seems to be an incredible case of excessive destruction. It must have been evident to the hunters of the day that numbers of specific animals were decreasing, especially if they were seen as a more desirable food source and thus sought out more keenly. And yet, everywhere that mega fauna existed throughout the planet, sooner or later it was brought to its knees. The only conclusion that seems to fit the picture is one of entitlement, a sentiment that has already been much in evidence. The animal kingdom was put there to feed Homo sapiens and any spiritual connection that might have existed between them as sentient beings was certainly overwhelmed if not totally obliterated.

By the time humanity had turned its attention from purely hunting and gathering in order to sustain itself, to the establishment of small communities based around agriculture, this may well have opened up an opportunity for more communion with the environment. Now plants and animals were being deliberately and conscientiously raised. It appears that the initial choice of crops that lent themselves to cultivation was quite limited. Likewise, only a few animal species seemed suitable for domestication. Settlers would have been drawn to the areas where the plants in question were already well established. Once the cultivation process had been understood, it is then likely that the settlers would have taken their newly acquired skills with them to other parts of the country in order to cultivate new areas and make provision for an expanding population. They would need to be mindful of the area selected to ensure that it would be supportive of their new farming processes. This would have necessitated an understanding of the environment in terms of soil fertility, rainfall, air and soil temperatures and extremes of weather that might be encountered. Obviously, these conditions could only have been appreciated through direct experience and so there would have been much trial and error. The initial transfer from Hunter gatherer to farmer and then the moving from one part of the country to another would have resulted in extreme hardship and possibly widespread death but it is most likely that this phase of human development led to a much greater understanding of the environment. Whether it extended to a level of spiritual communion is another matter. This was the beginning of the Agrarian Revolution. It lasted from some 9 or 10,000 years ago right up to the seventeenth century AD when it gave way to the Industrial Revolution.

There were several drivers that brought on this Revolution. Interestingly, the outcomes were not all positive and it is hard to see why farming endured without a closer study of the parallel social environment that was developing. While hunting and gathering appeared to be a relatively unregimented and casual life style, it would have been precarious in times of bad weather, animal herd migration, illness and even planetary climate change. The small communities that coexisted would have lived with these uncertainties, but looking backwards from today's ordered society, there must have been a fundamental attraction in the idea of staying in one place, cultivating known food crops and introducing a measure of order and control. Of course, natural events would have always interrupted such an imagined lifestyle, especially when a whole crop failed and the community was faced with starvation, or when another community that had experienced such a disaster had decided to take its neighbour's produce by force in order to survive. The initial work necessary to prepare the soil for planting, the clearing of other plants, small trees and weeds, the removal of rocks and stones, and the carriage of water to the site would all have been arduous, arguably far more so than the foraging and hunting which would not always have needed to be a daily event. Once the crop was planted, the daily care would have been relentless, and the anxiety associated with the potential for a wholesale loss of the harvest would have been present. There is little doubt that crop failures, illness and internecine warfare were all a reality for the early farming communities.

Despite the setbacks, they stuck with it and it became more widespread throughout the inhabited world. Community numbers supported by cultivation and animal husbandry rose to the low hundreds and where possible, some measure of crop and animal diversity was introduced. Although this did not compensate for the wide range of food that was available to the hunter gatherer, the fact that food was being produced in large quantities which would sustain over a hundred people was more appealing. The sense of community flourished and in time, a loose hierarchy developed within each settlement. Status would have come about based on the specific work that each community member performed. There would have been an inevitable and growing sense of order about living that did not exist with the hunter gatherers and it seems that this had the greater appeal. While the connectivity between humanity and its environment must have strengthened during this age, there is still no real tangible evidence that it existed on a spiritual level. Homo sapiens was at the top of the food chain, an apex animal and still able and willing to kill and ravage the countryside and its inhabitants at a whim.

Probably the level of human development that enshrined the most diverse sense of imagination arrived with the Mythic age. This is regarded as being first evident about the time of the Agrarian Revolution. It marked the early beginnings of the world's religions and saw the birth of a whole mythical universe full of gods and goddesses, monsters and demons all woven together in a rich panoply of story and myth. They were many and diverse. They held sway over humanity for thousands of years. Some remain extant to this day in a few communities of the world, while in other places they have been replaced or endorsed by religion.

The age hinged on Homo sapiens' ability to tell stories, to create imaginary pictures in their minds that could be described to others verbally in such a way that they became wholly believable. All this began long before the written word was available for the generation of books. The Mythic range was vast and covered everything from the dreamtime of the Australian aborigine, to the gods and goddesses of the Greek and Roman Empires, to the mythical monsters of the forbearers of the Scandinavian countries, to the mythical villains and heroes of the New Zealand Maori, to the many religions of the world. It is postulated that this ability to tell stories marked the great difference between Homo sapiens and other Homo erectus species that inhabited earth. One of the most noteworthy was the Neanderthal[2] who originated from the Neander Valley in what is Eastern Africa today. The species was widespread across Africa and Asia and was arguably more physically robust. However, it eventually succumbed and only sapiens endured.

There are many myths and religions which purported to support the environment, nature, flora and fauna, whatever description might suit. However, it appears that none has achieved any particular traction in their stated or implied objective. Humanity has simply continued throughout its time on the planet to use the environment as it thinks fit. Although the Agrarian Revolution saw the beginning of an intense human/nature interface which would last up to the present day, once again, it was for humanity's benefit and not nature's. Trees were still felled whenever and wherever it was deemed necessary, wild flowers, undergrowth, wetlands were all cleared or drained in like manner. When conflict struck, particularly during the two World Wars of the last century, the environment took yet another beating. This time it was necessary to enhance crop production both in terms of the individual plants and the density of planting. Food was in scarce supply as one faction of humanity tried to deprive the other of it in order to exercise its dominance and win the war. So the crop producing fields of the world began to be laced with chemicals to enhance production. Some were deemed to be naturally occurring, such as phosphates and nitrates and so they were added to the soil without any concern for either the short or long term consequences. Others were recognised as being less environmentally friendly but their use was equally casual. It was only much later that it was appreciated that the fine balances that existed in the producing soils had been upset. In addition, it was only subsequently realised that these excess chemicals would eventually move from the soils into the natural drainage systems of the countryside, the rivers. Here, they began to play havoc with the natural balance of the water resulting in widespread pollution and the loss of yet more species of the animal kingdom.

Near the coast, particularly in Australia great tracts of offshore coral reef began to show signs of pollution and widespread damage. These chemical cocktails were further enhanced by excessive animal waste from intensive farming which found its way into the rivers and the sea. While there was perhaps justification for the intensification of farming to meet a wartime need for higher production, there was no requirement for it to be maintained. However, by then the additional revenue to be earned from intensive farming had become the norm and was suitably attractive to the material based capitalist societies of the late twentieth and early twenty-first centuries. Towards the end of the twentieth century, there was a move towards organic farming, and this was to be applauded. It was presented as something new and retail shops that sold farming produce immediately 'jumped on the proverbial bandwagon' starting to segregate organic produce from the regular stocks so that more money could be charged for it. This was indeed capitalist cynicism in its finest form. It resulted in great damage being done to a noble movement which deserved and deserves better. In its most elementary form, organic farming comprises the growing of crops without the use of chemicals either for growth enhancement or the eradication of weeds. A certain reduction in yield is to be expected and therefore, there would appear to be justification for a higher price being required for the crop when it reaches its market. However, that is only a very small part of the picture. Organic farming is infinitely more complex than that and if carried out thoroughly and efficiently its yields, year on year can surpass any other form of farming. It does require dedication from the farmer and a level of empathy with nature and the environment that has been sadly lacking.

During the 'war years', yield per acre was everything. Pre-war there was less concern. Pre-war fields were invariably contained by hedgerows. A natural strip of eight or ten feet used to lie fallow all around the edge of the field. During the war years, this strip was ploughed, planted and cropped. The flora and fauna of the hedgerow suffered, depriving many insect and animal species of their food supply and basic life cycle. The crop spilled over to the edge of the field and during rains, precious soil and any chemical additives would be washed off into the laneways or roads. Weeds would creep in freely from the edge of the field invading the crop space. By reverting to a nature strip of ten to twelve feet and foregoing that land for cultivation, the hedgerows were revitalised, the natural flora and fauna returned aiding the natural balance and reintroducing pollination of adjacent growth. Soil erosion during heavy rain was eliminated and weed growth was less inclined to invade the crop. A thousand years before this, crop rotation had been used widely by most farming communities. This was a simple process whereby different plants were rotated through fields on an annual basis. Every few years a field would be allowed to lie fallow without a crop in order for the soils to enjoy some natural regeneration. By rotating crops, it would be possible to enhance the soils still further. Some plants have an ability to overproduce their own chemicals, typically nitrates. By rotating this crop with another that is in need of nitrate enhancement and the requirement for adding nitrates artificially has been removed. This process was possibly not fully understood by Norman Britain, but it was used extensively. Today, it is understood very well and is a substantial arrow in the organic farmer's quiver. This is just a very brief overview of a single element of such farming practise. There are many more. However, it is evident that all is not lost in terms of human/nature empathy.

The stories that humanity has learnt to tell itself are myriad. They have provided both the glue and the explosive material that has variously kept humanity together or blown it apart. Too often, the stories are flawed either because of a lack of knowledge or because of more direct manipulation. This was and still is the case with organic farming and the more widely recognised 'Green Movement'. Today, many democracies have 'Green Parties' supposedly supporting the environment in preference to the promotion of capitalism and a free-market economy. It is very difficult to differentiate well intentioned, empathetic behaviour based on sound philosophical principles from the more traditional self-serving populist presentations so many politicians hide behind. In much the same way, the organic movement has been politicised and misrepresented to its detriment. Suffice to say that the true and honest exponents of the principles and practises behind it, rather than those who serve only to support the movement as long as it is to their monetary or political advantage are the ones who deserve the accolades.

So far attention has been concentrated onshore. There is, of course another dimension to the abuse the planet and its ecosystems have suffered and that is offshore. Humankind has been fishing since the early days of its hunter gatherer phase. Initially, this would have involved simply catching fish by hand in shallow water. Shell fish would have been straightforward to collect and their residue has been found inland at recognised places of very early habitation. Until blue water ships and boats were conceived and built, the fish of the oceans were fairly safe from the marauding Homo sapiens. Although one species was singled out in the eleventh century by the Europeans: the Northern Right Whale. It was hunted and killed for its oil which could be burnt in a lamp to provide light. The flesh of the whale would have provided a source of protein and as time went on, more body parts and fluids found their way into soap, cosmetics, and other chemicals such as glycerine for explosive manufacture. But it wasn't until the Dutch, Norwegians and the British had caught on to the value contained in a whale carcase, that the industry began to really boom. Early whaling was carried out from sailing ships, but these gave way to steam driven vessels in the late nineteenth century. It had been realised early on that there were many other species of whale other than the Northern Right that were to prove profitable for hunting. By the early twentieth century, the world realised that it was yet again on the cusp of destroying an entire animal species and the brakes were applied. However, great damage had been done by then and it has been only by a huge international effort that a total disaster has been avoided, at least for the moment.

While there is ample evidence of the Romans and other societies of that period of history fishing in seagoing vessels, the really high intensity activities took off in the late eighteenth century and continue to this day. Just as whaling had become a global phenomenon, so the industrialised fishing industry followed suit which led to the indiscriminate plundering of fish stocks by all the nations whose territories bordered the oceans and seas of the world. Once again, multiple species were reduced to extraordinarily small numbers before there was any coordinated effort to limit fishing and avoid complete extinction. Today, offshore territorial fishing rights are a constant bone of contention between neighbouring states, partly because many people's livelihoods are seen to be at stake and any solution always comes with significant political overtones. However, the natural world has been saved from the wholesale slaughter of its fish stocks, again, for the moment.

There is another dimension to the exploitation of the offshore animal kingdom and that is through the industry that established itself to provide 'Offshore Big Game Fishing'. This is almost certainly a hangover from the Colonial days of the late nineteenth and early twentieth century when land-based Big Game Hunting was in its heyday. Fortunately, this is an activity which has been largely outlawed, although it has yet to be expunged completely. The origins of both activities may be buried in the need to fish or hunt for food but it is more likely that the real motivator has been a human desire to dominate while, at the same time, engage in something vaguely related to sport. The land based activity still has its proponents who happily shoot what are euphemistically referred to as 'Game birds'. These include both pheasants and grouse which are to be found in the countryside of the UK. Some are reared for the express purpose of being shot by hunting parties. Others are enjoying their natural habitat, where, at certain times of the year they become 'fair game' to be hauled out of the sky by hunters with shotguns. It is now a pastime that is quite well regulated and does not pose the threat of extinction to the bird species involved. However, it remains a sad indictment on humanity that considers such behaviour meritorious of the soubriquet 'sport'.

As far as 'Big Game Hunting' is concerned, that has been largely stamped out. However, this outlawing has only occurred relatively recently and the state of many target animals in terms of their ultimate viability as a species remains parlous. It is more than likely that other species will become extinct in the next 20 years simply because the numbers have been allowed to drop below the level of viability. 'Big Game Fishing' by contrast is alive and well. While it probably doesn't deplete fish stocks to any significant degree, it is a sad sight to see half a dozen six foot long sharks hanging from the gunwales of a game boat on its return to port after a day's fishing. As with the sport of pulling game birds out of the sky with a shotgun has, at best dubious associations with sport, so chasing down a free-swimming shark in open water with a large motorised vessel, attracting it to bite on a baited hook hanging over the side of the vessel and then wrestling it with a rod and line up to the side of the boat where it can be gaffed has equally little to do with sport. Sadly, the need to dominate another species prevails. It is both sad and extraordinary the lengths that humanity will still go to in order to mask such apparently primeval behaviour.

Arguably, it is only the great philosophers and sages of humanity, some of whom arrived on the scene well over 2,000 years ago in the middle of the Mythic Age who have given any real insight into the behaviours that might be more appropriate and acceptable for Homo sapiens as an animal species. Sadly, their works now do little more than adorn the shelves of academia and yet buried in their pages is the guidance and wisdom that humanity needed so desperately at the time of writing and needs even more today to avoid continuing on the path of the destruction of its environment and ultimately, itself. The animal kingdom has had something of a reprieve over the more recent past. Of course, it is all too late for a huge number of now extinct species but there has been some learning in other areas. In most instances, this seems to have been driven by a select few who have demonstrated a measure of empathy, if not with the animals themselves then with the rest of humanity. By their actions, the joy and richness of the environment is being preserved for future generations. But unless and until this compassion becomes widespread and is able to subsume the baser instincts that surround the elitism and hierarchical dominance of human beings over their animal kin, then the future remains bleak.

Chapter Seven
The Underdeveloped Human

In Plato's 'Republic',[1] he describes what he sees as humankind's condition more than 2,000 years ago. His description is set against a backdrop of an imagined philosophical discussion between a master and his pupils. The purpose of the discussion is to decide exactly what comprises the ideal arrangement for a new city assuming the planning is beginning from 'scratch' and there are no preconditions to be satisfied other than those that already exist as the essence of humanity. While the structure and language of the thesis suffers from the inevitable dulling or flattening associated with a translation combined with the relatively stilted sentence structure of Ancient Greek when compared with twenty-first-century prose, the behavioural descriptions of the city's intended inhabitants are unnervingly familiar. They are as alive and relevant today as they were in Plato's time. How on earth can this be the case when well over two thousand years of humankind's most dramatic period of development separates the two? The answer to this is perhaps more obvious than it is realised. While humanity has advanced itself dramatically in terms of its grasp and use of scientific discovery and technology, it has remained largely frozen in time in terms of its empathetic and spiritual growth. In fact, it could even be argued that it has regressed!

Much of the substance of the Mythic Age of Plato's time has gone, but by no means all of it. Science has been able to offer hypothesis after hypothesis followed up by observational proofs to explain the many cosmic and earthly phenomena which had hitherto been the embodiment of story or myth. Ironically, the recent staggering advancements in communication and information technology have placed 'knowledge' at the fingertips of everyone who has access to an electronic device capable of receiving and then re-transmitting this information. This has resulted in what could be defined as a pandemic but not of physical illness but of conspiracy. Huge numbers of anxious, often inadequately educated people who are faced with a world of increasing complexity and who are bombarded with endless, often heavily opinionated information have been left to their own devices to create stories and fantasies for themselves to deal with this suffocating environment in which they are now wholly immersed and yet have little understanding of. It is not the beginning of another Mythic Age but more a reflection of what little spiritual progress humankind has been able to make. Admittedly, the religions of the last two millennia have helped with some of the debunking of the Age and yet, many of these religions have been responsible for the substitution of their own myths and stories in order to explain the earthly philosophies of their belief, often by allegory.

The experience of fast and efficient global travel has been made available to large parts of the world's population. Extraordinarily sophisticated communication is available across the globe and with it the ability to both inform and mislead. In many countries, great attention has been paid to establishing welfare systems to care for the sick or less well disposed. Epidemic disease, once the bane of civilisation has been largely eradicated and worldwide procedures for the containment of pandemics are now tried and tested. Both world and local trade in goods and services has been long established and now operates with a high degree of success. But despite all of these advances, humanity remains divided by country, ethnicity, religion, and prejudices. Even though two World Wars have been endured, there are still many leaders, some of whom have been elected by democratic mandate who continue to believe their own often elaborate stories which provide them with the justification for the entitlement they enjoy. This sense allows the threat of war to be used freely and in some cases, enacted.

The idea of empathetic and spiritually based behaviour is not new. In many cultures and countries of the world, this has been enshrined since the time of Plato, if not before. This is not to be confused with the religious concept of Spirituality which, while having some similarities, came sometime after the writings of Plato and other gifted ancient sages and philosophers but which sadly has suffered manipulation and abuse to advance the wellbeing and entitlement of its various leaders. While predominantly evident in the East, Western philosophical thinkers have long been attracted to the writings, teachings and associated way of life of a spiritually based existence. But because the globe has been split down its north/south axis, largely as a result of the early imbalance of technological and practical development which seemed to foster pronounced prejudice and racial demarcation, the influence that the Eastern cultures have had over the so-called 'First world' of the West has been limited. Access to these cultures, by their very essence has always been open but has only been taken up by those who have been sufficiently curious or already enlightened. It is true that the West has shown more interest in the last 50 years, and Yoga, mindfulness and other meditative practises have been recognised and have become more acceptable in Western Cultures but despite this, the fundamental teachings have remained on the fringes. As is so often the case in Western Culture, new teachings, beliefs, radical or even simple new concepts all tend to breeze into and then out of fashion. They are just another 'fad', another idea or item of clothing to be championed or worn, a new diet, a new but different pair of legwarmers.

Perhaps even worse is the proliferation of experts who are now able to opine on every matter under the sun. These opinions appear in the written word via the Internet and so automatically have the associated authority humanity so willingly gifts to such presentations. The addition of contemporary photographic 'evidence' to support the proclaimed thesis imprints the theme in the mind of the reader still more firmly. Sadly, many of these publications are presented by people who hold some educational qualification in the particular field but for the sake of simplifying a complex subject, elect to precis or condense it and in the process, change the very essence of the conclusions. The idea of Mindfulness has been launched on the Western World over recent years. There is no doubt that the concept has value although, the very act of condensing what is a complete way of life into sessions of a few minutes a week, seems to show a level of contempt rather than one of empathy and understanding. It is even less surprising then to read accounts by other proclaimed psychologists and experts that this shortened process can actually be harmful in some situations. Just another pair of legwarmers by a different name.

Returning to Plato's 'Republic', there is a passage in the argument for the development, structure and behaviour of the ideal city where he makes extraordinary use of allegory. It has been referenced countless times but this has only enhanced its relevance. In it he deals with the subject of 'goodness', a third dimension or essential component and consequence of what is just and beautiful[2]. He and his pupil, Glaucon are discussing their idea of the necessary qualities of those who are to guard and govern the city and they conclude that it is no use in having such a person in that position who is unable to appreciate that things that are just and beautiful must also be good. Plato then prevaricates about describing the essence of 'Good' to Glaucon but instead agrees with him to discuss what he describes as 'The offspring of the good', something which is not good itself but which 'Bears a very close resemblance to it'. He then sets some other ground rules which the pair of them have talked about earlier in their discussions. He reminds him that they have already talked about there being many beautiful things and there being many good things and that distinguishing between them is achieved by the way they are talked about. Then there is beauty itself and good itself, each of which is referred to as a single form of itself i.e. 'what is beautiful' or 'what is good'. Now, he reminds Glaucon that something being beautiful or something being good is simply seen and not necessarily grasped by the intellect but, those things that are referred to as forms are grasped by the intellect and not seen. Finally, to reinforce his direction of travel, Plato asks Glaucon what sense it is that allows things to be seen to which Glaucon replies that it is sight.

Plato then introduces Glaucon to the idea that objects and vision alone are not enough for the visible senses to work, there has to be a third component. With hearing, a functioning pair of ears and a sound are sufficient ingredients, the concept of sound waves requiring something to travel through was not grasped for another three hundred years after Plato's writing. That discovery would not have undermined his logic as presented here because he could simply have chosen 'touch' as another sense requiring only two components to make his point. Glaucon then adds light to the equation of the visible senses. Interestingly, Plato asks Glaucon, "Which of the gods in the heavens do you take to be in charge of this?" to which Glaucon responds that it is the sun thus demonstrating that Mythic belief is alive and well even though the level of philosophical discussion is way ahead. The discussion continues with Plato stating that the sun is not sight itself but merely a facilitator of it but that it requires sight for the sun to be seen. And this is what Plato explains as the allegory of the offspring of the good. "The sun which the good fathered in proportion to itself: as the good itself is, in the sphere of the intelligible, in relation to intellect and the things that are grasped by intellect, so the sun is in the visible sphere in relation to sight and the things that are seen." This then leads Plato to draw a distinction between bright sunlight, semi-darkness and darkness which is relieved by an artificial lamp. In all three examples, the level of visual acuity varies, and the objects seen by the beholder thus assume different proportion and detail. In the same way, "When the soul directs itself towards something lit by the rays of truth, and towards what is, it grasps and recognises it at once, and it appears to possess intelligence; but when it directs itself at what comes into being and passes away, mingled as that is with darkness, it can manage no better than beliefs, its power weakening as these move up and down, this way and that, just like something of no intelligence at all."

Plato then completes the picture: "What provides things that are known with their truth, and gives the knower his proper capacity to know, this you can say is the form of the good itself. You should certainly think of it as something that is known; but as a cause of knowledge and truth, however beautiful both of these may be, you need to think of the good as different from and still more beautiful than they are. And just as in the parallel case we had to treat light and sight as resembling, but not as actually being, the sun, so here we need to treat knowledge and truth as resembling good, but neither of them as being good, because what the good is, in itself, is to be valued even more than they are."

Plato's presentation and language might be somewhat prosaic but what he has achieved here is to set out and record a fundamental concept that there was more to the human inhabitants of planet Earth than their simple presence and their ability to recognise, modify and manipulate physical material for their own ends. Even 2,500 years ago, before the widespread adoption of any of the recognised religions of today, there were those who had an understanding and appreciation of a higher level of thought than was necessary to simply eek out an existence. It was the attainment of this level of thinking that was problematic in Plato's time and is no different today.

His discussion with Glaucon continues as he broaches the subject of how this higher level of spiritual vision can be reached, maintained and passed on to others, for as he points out, there is little purpose in requiring the rulers of the new city to have these attributes if there are no teachers and there is no environment for them to learn in. Plato asks Glaucon to imagine a cave with a wide mouth some distance away from where the cave dwellers are located[3]. The dwellers have been there from birth and know only this environment. The mouth is a source of intense light, but it simply plays on the back of the dwellers as they are constricted in their movements by chains and can only look into the depths of the cave where everything is in shadow. Between the dwellers and the mouth of the cave is a long path going from one side of the cave to the other. It has a low wall such that only the upper part of everything that uses the path can be seen above the wall. As the dwellers cannot turn around, all they ever see of what passes across the cave is the shadow of the upper half cast onto the back wall of the cave by the light outside. Nothing has colour, depth or vibrancy, features normally associated with illumination by the sun, instead, everything is monochromatic, dark and two dimensional. Those that cross the path carry with them every conceivable manufactured item, statues of humans, books, lamps, thing made of metal, things made of wood, furniture, water fountains, the list is endless. Sometimes they talk but because the dwellers cannot see them but only their shadows, they have to assume that the sound comes from the shadows rather than that which cast them. Once Plato has painted this picture, Glaucon comments that it seems like a strange picture with strange prisoners to which Plato replies that it is "One that resembles us."

Next, Plato asks Glaucon to imagine that one of the prisoners is released. His manacles are removed, and he is free to stand up, turn around and look out of the mouth of the cave into the light. At first, he would be confused and overwhelmed by its intensity. If he was interrogated at that point by one of his erstwhile jailers and asked which was real and which was illusory, he would select his lifetime's experience of the shadows as reality. If he was then offered the opportunity to walk out of the cave towards the light he would almost certainly prefer to bolt back into the cave, to familiarity where the light didn't burn his eyes and the picture of two different images of the same object confused him. But if he was dragged from the cave physically, and set down outside in the sunshine, slowly he would acclimatise to its intensity, initially being able to look into its reflection in water and finally summoning the courage to look directly at the substantial source of his own vision. He would see the depth and dimension of all that passed before him, the colours and the subtle shapes. He would hear the spoken word and identify where it came from. At night, he would lie beneath the stars and marvel at the vision above. Eventually, he would be offered the chance to return to the cave of his upbringing and his adult life. To return would result in him having to be manacled once more, to peer through the half-light at only the shadowy forms of what he now knows is reality. His eyes would be slow to accommodate to the gloom and he would be ridiculed by his peers for his loss of ability in this half world. Once making the transition out of the cave, it seems that there is little incentive to return.

And so Plato continues with his rather stark analogy. It is not difficult to match the images he draws of the two environments with society then or now. When he and Glaucon discuss who would be the better city rulers, those who have accepted life manacled in the cave and who have created innumerable stories and fantasies in order to sustain themselves in such a dimensionless environment, or those who have had the courage and the innate wisdom to see beyond it and to venture outside, there is no debate. However, there is a challenge that remains and that is how to school those still in the cave. Who would want to return having seen the light, and be faced with the task of convincing those of less courage and wisdom to make the journey? Once a philosopher has attained a level of spiritual equilibrium it is unusual for a society to encourage him or her to take a different route. But there is no doubt that in Plato's city this must be an acceptable occupation for the good of all. Those who have made the journey simply cannot abandon their kith and kin. They have a moral and spiritual duty to either put themselves forward as guards and city rulers or to take on the task of identifying and teaching those who will follow.

In this snapshot of Plato's Republic, it is hopefully evident that there was an understanding of the higher levels of spiritual attainment accessible by humankind well over 2,000 years ago. What hasn't been mentioned is that Socrates, Plato's teacher and mentor was tried for corrupting youth, worshipping false gods and not worshipping the state religion. His trial was against a backdrop of great state and political upheaval where Athens was swinging between democratic and dictatorial governments having just lost a significant naval battle against the Spartans. Socrates was found guilty and eventually put to death by the administration of poison despite being offered many olive branches beforehand. While the detailed analysis of the reason for his initial summons and his eventual demise is interesting and the subject of much historical speculation, the simple fact that the state found his very existence sufficiently challenging to warrant his execution is probably more revealing about Athenian society and its very confidence. History shows that innumerable societies right up to the present day have been greatly troubled by original thinkers. Their usual modus operandi is to publicly discredit them, trump up appropriate corruption charges or worse, try them and then either sentence them to death or deport them to a Gulag. Historically, these sorts of behaviours have often related to the various religions of the world. If it is not a conflict between state and religion, then it is a conflict within the religion itself. In nearly all cases, the status quo of the ruling elite has been challenged by perceived or actual anti state rhetoric or in the case of religion, by heresy. However, this is not the reason why humanity has been unable to elevate its thinking to a higher level of spiritual appreciation and understanding. That would seem to be more of a regional issue than a worldwide one for, as has been suggested already, the East has cultivated societies that are far more willing to embrace such thinking and practise to the extent that they have become the defining environments. But even in the East, systems of government, autocratic behaviours, wars and conflicts, both inter and intra state have all helped to limit the broader adoption of enlightened thinking.

As Plato points out during his discussion with Glaucon, there is not much appetite for the students of philosophy to embark on a political career. Once they have attained a genuine understanding of humankind's enormous spiritual capacity and have learnt to be at peace with themselves and the rest of nature, the erstwhile Earthly drivers such as wealth, position, status or the amassing of worldly goods fade to insignificance. And just as Plato suggested, to return to the cave and sit once more amongst the unenlightened who surround themselves with myth and story, squabble interminably as to whether the most recent shadow they saw passing their projected field of vision is the same as the one the day before or whether it is a more advanced version, is a burden they would rather not contemplate. And so the great majority of humanity has been denied the opportunity of leadership by the more balanced members of human society, those who have taken the time and energy to search for a greater meaning of life, a better more compassionate view of all other sentient beings and nature itself. Instead the sovereign states of the world continue to be under the control and management of those who have mastered living in the cave better than their contempories. These are the people who have yet to acknowledge and be able to release their more damaging pathologies, those residual elements of the states of mind that that all humans pass through as they grow and mature and which somehow have remained with them into adulthood.

Chapter Eight
From Plato to the End of the
Last Millennium

The study of philosophy and associated human behaviours is complex. By and large, it is not offered in Western schools and its uptake as a subject is not normally possible until tertiary levels of education are reached, unless of course a would-be student elects to set out on his or her own study. There are probably two main reasons for this. If its complexity and dimensionless form make it difficult to study, it will be challenging to teach and will not sit well with young students. But more importantly, if its history is traced back through to Plato's time, then it becomes apparent that it has had to share the stage with the development and adoption of the religions of the world. Philosophy and religion are uncomfortable bedfellows at the best of times and so while not disappearing completely during religions' dominance of nearly 2,000 years, the study and pursuit of philosophy as a subject in its own right as distinct from its implicit study associated with religious dogma tended to fade through this period.

There is little to be gained from pitting religion against philosophy. The relationship between the two is anything but straightforward. Philosophy seeks to understand humanity, its behaviours, its drivers, its pathologies, its purpose and its place amongst the Earth's diversity of flora and fauna, sometimes referred to as Nature. Unlike the religions of the world, it does not need a god-head for it to exist. It does not need a story to support the arrival of the godhead, be it Allah in the Seventh Century AD, Jesus in the First Century AD, or Judaism's Yahweh in 2,000 BCE. There are many other ancient religions that pre-date Judaism and each has played a part or continues to play a part in humanity's journey from the Neander Valley and its other cradles to the present day. They have all influenced humankind's development, sometimes positively and other times less so. While the very stories that sustain them have been of enormous benefit to humankind in helping it to come to terms with adversity, hardship, loss or simply coping with the daily process of existing, they have also caused division, hatred, discontent and a profound distrust in the advancement of learning. Just where the scales of justice would sit if the good was balanced against the bad is another matter.

Yuval Harari presents a most plausible explanation for why Homo sapiens eventually stole the animal stage from all the other Homo erectus species in his historical book on humanity, *Homo Sapiens*[1]. It is his well-argued conviction that the unique ability of story-telling that Homo sapiens mastered became the decisive factor in its rise to unchallenged supremacy amongst the other species. These stories became elaborate and often less than truthful. They facilitated groups to stick together as the subject of the stories would often have centred around food sources, location of wild animals or other potentially life controlling events. Nothing would have been written down at that time but that would not have prevented many of them being used repeatedly and passed from person to person. Today, stories continue to be a fundamental feature of humanity. Whereas they were once used to gain an advantage over another group in a food sourcing environment, possibly by fabricating the presence of a threatening wild animal when none was there, now they are used for everything from helping young children to go to sleep to the control and subjugation of whole societies. Their origin lies in the ability of the early Homo sapiens' mind to imagine a scene or a sequence of events that had not actually taken place but the mental image that was created was powerful enough to be represented in speech, possibly aided by the use of sign language or drawings, to enable it to be passed on. This ability suggests a significant development of that part of the brain allowing it to handle fantasy alongside the more regimented processes necessary simply to repeat an account of an event that had been recently witnessed. Whether or not this ability was the defining trait to be found in Home sapiens and not in other Homo erectus species, may be moot. However, it is a feature of all of humanity today and one which is of huge significance.

Whether a man called Jesus existed in the early part of the First Century AD does not really need to be contested. After all, the very calendar that much of Western society uses to ground its historical chronology on today is based on his supposed birth date. It is highly improbable that his life and teachings as recorded in Christian writings are a fabrication. To challenge them is somewhat akin to arguing the true identity of Shakespeare. Someone wrote his plays if it was not actually him. Whoever it was does not detract from the genius contained within their written words. And so it is with Jesus, his philosophical teachings as recorded are extraordinary and well worthy of permanent recognition in humanity's historical struggles with itself. Many of the parables he is accorded with authoring are as relevant in today's society as they were two thousand years ago. As a young man, his grasp of practical psychology and philosophy was extraordinary and even if he hadn't enjoyed anything other than very localised admiration during his lifetime, like so many gifted people their true talent does not become recognised and acknowledged until long after their demise. It is not difficult to appreciate Judaism's enthusiasm for embracing Jesus and everything that he meant to his followers as a part of their ongoing scriptures. Exactly when this happened is not necessarily important, but there is little doubt that it needed to be well established by the time Islam's Allah arrived on the scene.

The story of early Christianity takes place against the backdrop of the Roman Empire, a formidable societal and military force that had been extant for several hundred years and would remain so for another eight hundred. This empire was built in the Mythic Age[2] when humankind believed in gods and goddesses, demons and ghouls and countless myths and stories to go with them. It wouldn't be surprising for the proponents of Christianity to have taken advantage of some of this enthusiasm for story-telling and myth generation to enhance the importance and uniqueness of the earthly manifestation of their God. What harm could there be in according Jesus a Virgin birth, in him performing countless miracles in front of his ardent followers and finally for allowing him to be persecuted by the State, crucified, put to death, buried and then finally resurrected? All this may well have happened but the tragedy of these stories, if that is all that they are, is that they have overwhelmed something of much more worth and intrinsic value. Jesus' life was recorded as one of simplicity, conducted amongst ordinary people during which time he espoused profound philosophical wisdom to both young and old around him. His perceptions and grasp of humanity, its successes and shortcomings were profound and had a striking effect on all those who listened to him. Were the more elaborate stories simply constructed by the assumed leaders as a means of enhancing the perceived authenticity of the religion? That would be desperately sad. Regardless, there seems to be little doubt that his deification has served to both elevate and reduce the very essence of one of humanity's greatest philosophers.

While Christianity slowly spread beyond what is now referred to as the Middle East, it was also embedding itself in Rome. There were a number of emperors who declared themselves to be Christian. Although persecution of those who publicly supported religious faith was still very much in evidence, Christianity was making progress.

The gradual decline of the Roman Empire took some eight hundred years. It coincided with the emergence of Islam and the division of Christianity whereby some of the basic tenants were modified and Rome became the seat of power and influence for the resulting Latin Church. At the end of the eleventh century, there began the most alarming set of wars, the Crusades. They were fought in and around Jerusalem, the two armies representing Islam on the one side and Christianity on the other. They were brutal conflicts with one army marching for months from as far afield as Britain and what are now the northern countries of Europe in order to confront their foes on the battlefields. The cause of the wars was simple, 'our God is better than yours!' It was imperative that the 'Muslim hoards' be driven from the Holy land and the integrity of the one and only true religion be upheld. This was a repeated behaviour in one form or another right up into the seventeenth century. The first Crusades were the only ones to be fought in and around Jerusalem but subsequent religious based conflicts took place in what is now Turkey, Spain and the Balkan States. What a sad reflection on the level of humanity's development that it was reduced to physical violence as the only way to support and uphold something supposedly true and spiritually perfect.

While the world's churches were spreading their influence on societies, they continued to feed conflict. If they were not bickering internally, then they were challenging the State wherever they were based. Stories and myths continued to be a fundamental feature of their fabric. Management structures had long been established for each one and with some, the most senior representative was acknowledged as being their god's direct descendent. For the tens of millions of humans on the planet, most of whom had only the most rudimentary practical education, the hierarchy of their particular church was far more dominant and significant in their lives than local or state government. And yet, the churches declared that their role in society was principally to care for the spiritual health of their followers. Some religions were indifferent to the existence of others. They were at least prepared to acknowledge if not to actually accept the differences of their respective faiths. Others were not so accommodating as demonstrated by the more rigorous interpretation of Islam which in some countries still regards apostasy as a punishable crime, sometimes with the death sentence when the accused is supposedly guilty of abandoning Islam for another faith.

While the various faiths of the world maintained the levels of authority and control over their congregations that was felt necessary and appropriate, there were those independent thinkers who continued their philosophical studies and writings. However, much of it was overshadowed by theological dogma which relied on cultivating a climate of fear as the best means of controlling adherence to the faith. After the fall of the Roman Empire, much of Europe was subsumed by one barbarian invasion after another up until the First Crusade at the end of the eleventh century. Christianity began to re-establish itself only to be bowled over again by the Reformation. However, by the seventeenth century, scientific discovery and technology was beginning to dominate Western culture, particularly in Europe and Britain. This had the effect of loosening the monopoly that recognised religion had on society's idea of philosophical thought. In turn, this lead to the acknowledgement of those who were quite independent of theology, such as Descartes, being recognised not as a theologian but as a philosopher in his own right. Thereafter, there followed a succession of learned figures who developed a variety of theses in an attempt to accommodate humanity's dichotomy. Initially, much of the thinking was focused on the ego and it wasn't until Nietzsche and others of his generation appeared on the scene that the heroic view of humanity arrived. Even with this relatively newfound status, philosophy was still regarded as an intense subject, the exclusive domain of the most learned scholars, and so to most of the world, its output was largely obscured by the more popular news and events of the day. Despite this, the subject's rediscovery was solid and it would not be so easily concealed in the future. Much of the work of the most noteworthy philosophers of successive generations tended to reflect the social and political environment of the day but whenever significant scientific or technical advancement took place, this was usually accorded much more credit, if not at the time then in subsequent historical accounts. The philosopher, meanwhile, worked away quietly out of the limelight, his only audience being his philosophically thinking peers. Occasionally, when a fundamental clash appeared between philosophy and religion, then this caused a greater flurry of interest but it was seldom sustained.

When humanity found itself on the cusp of a new Millennium 20 odd years ago, it had reached a very interesting junction brought about by the staggering advancement in electronic communication, the Internet and a general liberalisation of most western societies, all of which conspired to shake establishments that were not thought to be shakeable and to herald a new order, one that would prove to be decidedly less stable.

With the exception of enduring centres of religious intensity such as the 'Bible Belt' of the USA, the somewhat autocratic sovereign states whose beliefs were firmly established in Catholicism and in all those countries where the Islamic faith was dominant, the years after the Second World War saw a marked decline in the influence of the Church on Western societies. With it came a gradual liberalisation of society, a move away from autocratic thinking, "We do it this way because we have always done it this way!" and the acknowledgement and elevation to majority status of minority groups in society who had hitherto either been marginalised or actually persecuted. These events were seen as being both progressive in terms of providing fair treatment for all and spiritually elevating because humanity's citizens were now being required, very often by legislation, to look at one another and behave in a neutral non-judgemental light. While society as a whole appears to have reacted positively to this wave of liberalism, it has dealt some of the established religious orders a series of severe blows to the body.

Religion in nearly all its forms has relied on largely unelected autocratic management. Control of congregations by love and fear in equal measure has prevailed. The rigour associated with the execution of a church's practises and procedures is followed scrupulously and the dogma of its scriptures is immutable. So when society begins to relax some of the Victorian and Edwardian behaviours, even in something as simple as appropriate dress codes for different societal events, then the Church is faced with a dilemma. Does it conform to modern trends or uphold its traditional values? Either option has a consequence, and neither is particularly palatable. Traditions are the very cornerstones of religions. To ask for change, especially when that change requires the church's establishment to shift its autocratic behaviour, is poking a stick at its very fabric. The consequence is simple; it results in a diminution, however small of the church's position in society. When the change championed by society is more fundamental and actually challenges one of the basic tenants of the Church's principles, then that same fabric is badly torn. The Church must somehow address what has now passed into statute at the hands of the state and either amend its thinking and its associated interpretation of its scriptures or add a codicil to one of its enshrined commandments that allows the matter to be 'fudged' and then turn a Nelsonian eye to whatever transpires as a future consequence. Despite these events, religious belief has prevailed even if the church has become less relevant in society today than it was 50 or even 20 years ago.

Meanwhile, the philosopher has continued to ply her trade. But now the world has opened up. Suddenly, anecdotal snippets can be put before huge numbers of people simultaneously across Social Media. Admittedly, these may not be extracts from Bertrand Russell's *History of Western Philosophy* nor the *Complete Works of Ken Wilber* but they are often derived from contemporary psychologists and part time philosophers who are eager to share their theories of raising children, comments on the behaviours of certain elements of society or almost anything that might be of some interest to those who frequent these media pages on their laptops, phones or other electronic devices. While the sharing of knowledge is precious and should be cultivated, it is a double edged sword as society has rediscovered. It was Alexander Pope[3] who pointed out in his poem entitled *An essay on criticism* which he wrote at the beginning of the eighteenth century, that 'A little learning is a dangerous thing'. Such compact truisms are to be found littering most modern languages and care should be taken with their application. In this case, Pope was discoursing on the matter of 'Criticism' and he was at pains to point out that it was important for the critic to read and be mindful of the whole of the subject work. In the same way, those seeking knowledge should 'drink deep or taste not the Pierian spring'. (The Pierian spring of Macedonia was sacred to the Pierides and the Muses in Greek Mythology as being the source of all knowledge of Art and Science). The relevance is clear, either study the subject in depth or be very cautious with (the application of) what superficial knowledge has been gleaned. Maybe this simple sentence should be a compulsory inscription at the beginning of each and every article posted on electronic media or else it might well end up as present day society's epitaph.

Chapter Nine
The Beginning of the Twenty-First Century

The consensus achieved between some of the more notable philosophers during the late twentieth and early twenty-first century has been quite remarkable. While there remains a wide diversity of opinion, the most notable being that between religious based theory and evolutionary theory, the work being done with developmental psychology, the study of the growth and development of the human mind is quite heartening. So much so that a number of leading figures in Western governments have endorsed programmes that are designed to embody significant concepts of philosophical thinking into their respective political processes. Work has also progressed on the practical aspects of being able to demonstrate visible evidence of a mind which is in a state of spiritual engagement. This is not science fiction but the product of proportionate and well managed medical and scientific investigation. Not only has it been successful with Western subjects, but it has also demonstrated an almost identical reaction in subjects from Eastern cultures which will be of benefit when trying to diminish the notion of cultural conditioning being at the route of any state of spiritual elevation. The state of mind being examined in this way can be thought of as that which Plato's prisoner embraced when she freed herself from the shackles which secured her in the cave and ventured outside to embrace the light and reality of the world.

In Ken Wilber's book, *A Theory of Everything*[1], he describes Developmental Psychology as, "The study of the growth and development of the mind—the study of interior development and conscious evolution." He then goes on to point out that, "One of the striking things about the present state of developmental studies is how similar, in broad outline, most of its models are." This suggests that there is a measure of consensus between the current and recent past leading theorists. Quoting again from *A Theory of Everything*, Wilber says[2], "From Clare Graves to Abraham Maslow; from Deidre Kramer to Jan Sinnott; from Jurgen Habermas to Cheryl Armon; from Kurt Fischer to Jenny Wade; from Robert Kegan to Susanne Cook-Greuter, there emerges a remarkably consistent story of the evolution of consciousness." If this is the case, then it is very encouraging that humanity may have finally homed in on a plausible broadly agreeable model for how modern society has reached the point that it has. Obviously, there will be detractors, those whose views differ wildly from basic premise to conclusion. There will also be a large number of disagreements and conflicts, especially over the details and the more subtle deductions of those theorists that have been referenced by Wilber. As he points out, none of it is perfect, and it will only stand as it is now until something else grows upwards and outwards from it.

The development path of the human mind and the way in which it behaves from the period of the hunter gatherer up to the present day has been referred to as the 'Evolution of consciousness'. It would seem that it is mirrored daily by the development of the human child as she moves from birth to adulthood. Interestingly, there is now a significant cohort of modern philosophical thinkers that has reached broad consensus over the models that have evolved to describe this enormously complex subject. This has all happened quite recently. The various models described are elegant. They are not linear and ladder-like in their progression but instead tend to rely on a certain fluidity for their connectivity, one level with another. In order to appreciate this, it is worthwhile quoting Clare Graves here as Wilber goes on to do in *A Theory of Everything*. Graves generated a model and of it he said,[3] "Briefly, what I am proposing is that the psychology of the mature human being is an unfolding, emergent, oscillating spiralling process marked by progressive subordination of older, lower order behaviour systems to newer, higher-order systems as an individual's existential problems change. Each successive stage, wave, or level of existence is a state through which people pass on their way to other states of being. When the human is centralised in one state of existence, he or she has a psychology which is particular to that state. His or her feelings, motivations, ethics and values, biochemistry, degree of neurological activation, learning systems, belief systems, conception of mental health, ideas as to what mental illness is and how it should be treated, conceptions and preferences for management, education, economics and political theory and practise are all appropriate to that state." (C. Graves: *Summary statement: The Emergent, Cyclical, Double-Helix Model of the Adult Human Biopsychosocial Systems* Boston, May 20, 1981). Graves suggested that there were eight discrete levels in his model, which accords with other similar models proposed elsewhere. These are not simply ideas that have been conceived and postulated. They have been researched and grounded with much collected evidence.

Don Beck and Christopher Cowan have taken Clare Graves's work forward in an approach they call 'Spiral Dynamics'[4]. As Wilbur explains, they have used the same eight general stages of development which they called memes. They have been colour-coded beginning with beige, followed by purple, red, blue, orange, green, yellow and turquoise *(See Figure 9.1 overleaf).* A ninth colour has been added, coral to reflect what some believe is a higher level now beginning to emerge in some human beings. Each stage or level aims to define or contain a level of conscious development that has been achieved within that group of people that occupy it. The edges of each stage are not precisely defined and the transition from one to another, while generally permanent does not mean that a lower or lesser stage cannot be revisited given certain existential experiences. The first stage, Beige represents the 'instinctual' level of humanity when it survived on instinct alone, an emphasis on little more than living to survive by whatever means. This is the basis of the hunter gatherer's earliest environment. It also represents the new born infant. The second stage, Purple is the age of animism or magical behaviours, the grouping together of small bands of people seeking harmony and safety in additional numbers. However, there is no connectivity outside the immediate tribe or family group. As far as the child is concerned, this equates to what Margaret Mahler[5] has referred to as 'the hatching' when the infant recognises that there is a division between his blanket and his thumb. It is the first concept of bodily-self beginning to emerge from everything else that is around him. The third stage, Red sees the emergence of the 'self' as distinct from the group or tribe to which each person has been historically attached. The magical of the Purple is now mixed with the Mythic of the Red. For the developing human, the world is now full of powerful beings, both good and bad. It is an opportunity to exploit others, to dominate or be dominated. For the child, she is now in the 'terrible twos' which most parents acknowledge as lasting well beyond that age. The fourth stage, Blue sees the beginning of a rigid social hierarchy with immutable principles of 'right' and 'wrong'. Life now has meaning and direction, even if it is strictly controlled by puritanical authority. It is seen in Dickensian England, Puritan America and

Confucian China. As for the human child, he is now in his early phase of appreciating that there are other points of view that may differ from his own and that he would do well to listen and adjust his thinking accordingly. The fifth stage, Orange is the age of scientific achievement and industrial development. The world is now organised and rational with natural laws that explain, can be learnt and then, with some, manipulated. It is the beginning of the age of materialism and individual wealth which can be sought and amassed by other than those who come from the privileged classes of the Blue stage. The child is now in her adolescent period.

Figure 9.1[1]. The Spiral Development

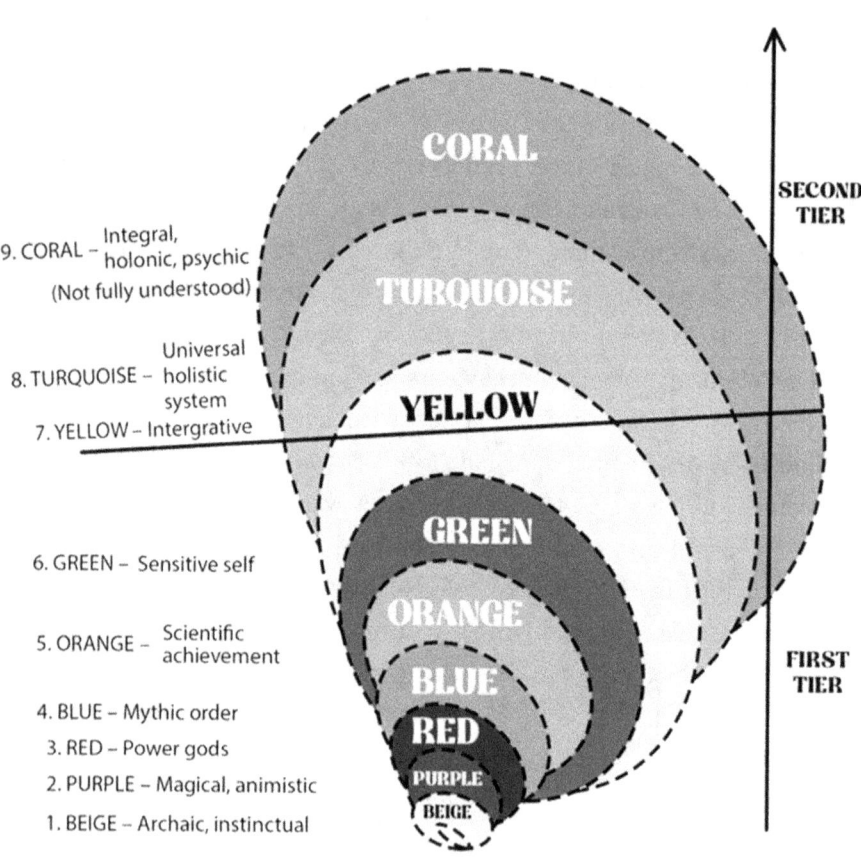

Ken Wilber, "A Theory of Everything". Page 8. Figure 1–1. Shambhala Publications, Boulder, Colorado, USA, Published 2001.

The next stage, Green is the last one if humanity is to remain at the mechanistic, essentially non-spiritual phase of evolution. In it, humankind has developed a measure of mutual bonding within its own ranks. It has tried and succeeded in breaking away from dogma and to a lesser extent, greed, both essential steps before any further upward movement is possible. Decisions are now reached by consensus, although this often results in less than optimal processes and outcomes. Society tries to be strongly egalitarian and anti-hierarchical. Minority groups are afforded the same if not greater recognition and authority as the majority. Society has embraced much of what is required to launch itself upwards but it remains shackled to only one dimensional views of its environment, its relationships with others and the overall concept of hierarchy which rightly continues to define everything that is known and understood about the Kosmos, the Ancient Greek's word to describe the earth, the heavens and everything known, the patterned nature or process of all domains of existence.

Before addressing the remaining memes or stages of Spiral Dynamics, it may be helpful to add some important but complicating material to the picture of evolutionary development. Ken Wilber, who is generally regarded as one of the leading American philosophers of the twentieth and twenty-first centuries, utilises a model for the Kosmos[6] which represents it in four quadrants[7]. He does not take credit for the origin of the model but he is at pains to point out the significance of the word Kosmos. Its origin lies with the Pythagoreans of Ancient Greece and its original meaning was "the patterned nature or process of all domains of existence, from matter to math to theos, and not merely the physical universe, which is usually what both 'cosmos' and 'universe' mean today." Expanding on the definition a little further, it can be deduced that the Kosmos actually contains the cosmos, which is simply the physical component or 'physiosphere', one of the domains of existence, and the other three domains, sometimes known as the bios or biosphere, the nous or noosphere, and the theo or theosphere. Returning to the four quadrants, they can be visualised as being part of a large square, with four diagonal lines from the common centre outwards, to the nearest corner of the square *(See Figure 9.2 overleaf)*. Thus, the diagonal lines represent the development path of each quadrant. In the presentation of Clare Graves Spiral Dynamics, Don Beck and Christopher Cowan began the series with the Beige meme which would accord with the first point on the diagonal line of the quadrant dealing with the Self and consciousness, the 'I', the Upper Left. The next point will be the Purple and so on all the way up and out to the Yellow and Turquoise. This quadrant, sometimes referred to as UL (for Upper left) because that's the position it is in on the diagrammatic view, represents the interior of the individual, what he or she is conscious of. Although it only contains a single diagonal line, that line represents the waves or stages of interior development which embrace everything from matter to body to mind to soul and to spirit. While it is sequential, it is anything but lineal. If the spiral of Figure 9.1 is superimposed on the diagonal line of the UL, it may help to appreciate the breadth and depth of each phase rather than thinking of each as just a point on a line.

If the Upper Right or UR quadrant is now considered, it is tracing the physical or external view, the 'It' of each stage on the UL, the brain and organisms. Consequently, it has the organic states of the human brain but first, it begins with atoms then molecules then prokaryotes then eukaryotes then neuronal organisms then neural chord then reptilian brain stem, the limbic system and finally on out to the Structure Functions of the brain. This demonstrates the importance of considering both the internal and not necessarily visible components of something and the external view of the same thing as they present two very different but complimentary views. Both are critically important but give a very different, incomplete and potentially distorted account of matters when viewed alone and assumed as being representative or equivalent of both.

Figure 9.2[2]. Some Examples of the Four Quadrants in Humans

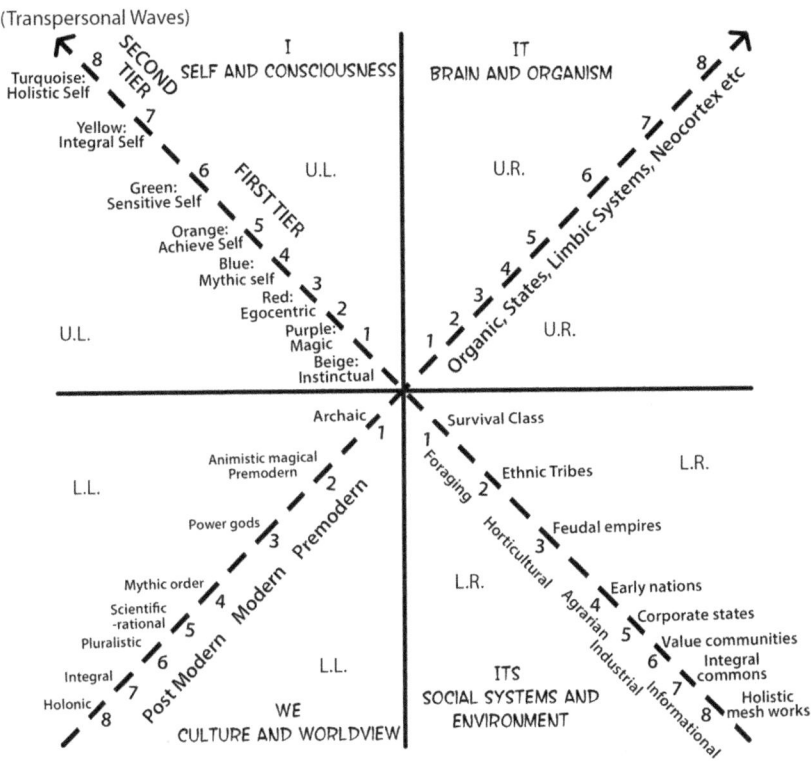

Ken Wilber, "A Theory of Everything". Page 43. Figure 3–1. Shambhala Publications, Boulder, Colorado, USA, Published 2001.

The two lower quadrants in Wilber's diagram Lower Left, LL and Lower Right, LR trace the Interior Collective or Cultural and worldview, the 'We' and the Exterior Collective or Social systems and environment, the 'Its' of the Kosmos. In the LL, the Cultural or worldview, he traces the defining stages that build the cultural component of humanity which can be identified as beginning with the Archaic and then the Animistic or magical, the Power gods, the Mythic order, the Scientific or rational, the Pluralistic, the Integral and the Holonic. The levels across all four quadrants are effectively matched or balanced with one another and thus the Pluralistic and Integral stages represent the collective group behaviours or status of the interior Green and Yellow stages of the individual in

89

the UL. Wilber sometimes refers to these two colours as 'formal-operational' and 'vision-logic', of the individual in the UL. They will become very significant and central to the story. The final quadrant LR, tracing the Exterior Collective or Social systems and environment, begins with the identification of the Survival class of humanity, the early hunter-gatherer and then onto Ethnic tribes, Feudal empires, Early nations, Corporate States, Value communities, Integral commons, and Holistic networks. This quadrant can be described as the Social component of the LL. It is an expansion of the more recognisable historical stages that may be familiar, namely Foraging, Horticultural, Agrarian and Industrial. In terms of equivalence, in the Interior Collective or Cultural and worldview LL levels, the Scientific rational and Pluralistic accord with the Corporate states and Value communities of the LR. Another way of visualising the quadrants is to refer to each by its appropriate pronoun, and thus, the UL is the 'I', the UR is the 'It', the LL is the 'We' and the LR is the 'Its'.

It should be pointed out that the Four Quadrant model here is incomplete. It has been depicted as beginning at the level of the arrival of the earliest human beings in order to accommodate only their evolution. There are earlier stages that appear in all quadrants which begin with Prehension in UL, Atoms in UR, Physical-pleromatic in LL and Galaxies in LR and which accord with the perceived 'beginning of time'. While the full presentation is more thorough, it is probably more confusing than helpful at this stage. A more complete appreciation of the model can be found in Ken Wilber's *Sex, Ecology and Spirituality*.

Behind Wilber's Four Quadrants model lies the concept of hierarchy. The agreement with and the acceptance of this thesis which accounts for the entire Kosmos is hugely significant if humanity is to succeed in lifting itself to the Yellow stage, the first of second tier or spiritual thinking. The concept is very straightforward but is met with unwavering resistance and outright dismissal from many sections of society. This is deeply worrying as it is such a fundamental principal which is enshrined throughout nature and the environment. It is nothing more than the basis for the *science of wholeness* or *Systems Theory* as Wilber states in his early chapters in *Sex, Ecology and Spirituality*[8]. 'The Great Chain of Being' saw matter, body and mind as a vast network of mutually interweaving orders subsisting in Spirit, with each node in the continuum of being, each link in the chain, being absolutely necessary and intrinsically valuable. This owes its origins to Socrates and, with the obvious religious exceptions were the defining concept of evolution and the associated development of planet Earth as a part of the Kosmos right up until the 1700s. Unfortunately, the theory was ruptured during the rise of modern science and it wasn't until late in the twentieth century that the rupture was repaired. Its origin lay in the differential development of the physical sciences over that three hundred year period. Without going into great detail, suffice to say that an incomplete grasp of the relationship between time, the material world, Newtonian mechanics and Thermodynamics was responsible for the damage. Some very fundamental rules linking these elements together which had been teased out by observation, investigation, and experimentation had appeared to contradict each other in a very fundamental way suggesting that parts of the Kosmos were in irreversible decay while others were constantly evolving. It wasn't until late in the twentieth century that these anomalies were ironed out, not completely, but sufficiently to demonstrate that there were no gaping holes in the basic Systems Theory.[9]

There is no doubt that the concept of hierarchies has been embraced by a broad church. Quoting again from Ken Wilber's *Sex, Ecology and Spirituality* to gain an idea of just how universally acknowledged this is, he says,[10] "Here are the actual system sciences talking openly and glowingly of hierarchy. The founder of General Systems Theory, Ludwig von Bertalanffy ('Realty, in the modern conception, appears as a tremendous hierarchical order of organised entities') to Rupert Sheldrake and his 'nested hierarchy of morphogenetic fields'; from the great systems linguist Roman Jakobson ('Hierarchy, then, is the fundamental structural principle of language') to Charles Birch and John Cobb's ecological model of reality based on 'hierarchical values'; from Francisco Varela's groundbreaking work on autopoietic systems ('It seems to be a general reflection of the richness of natural systems…to produce a hierarchy of levels') to the brain research of Roger Sperry and Sir John Eccles and Wilder Penfold ('A hierarchy of nonreducible emergents') and even in the social critical theory of Jurgens Habermas ('A hierarchy of communicative competence')—hierarchy seems to be everywhere."

Sadly, for humanity the consensus amongst the sages, thinkers and philosophers is not as complete as it might be. Historically, the word hierarchy implied bigger, better, more powerful, and invariably more discriminatory, especially towards minorities. For those that oppose the concept, it is a simple step to apply the somewhat semantic thinking as a means of dismissing hierarchies altogether as they belong in the 'dark ages'. While any system that relies on discriminatory behaviour as a part of its justification is quite obviously inappropriate, it is equally disingenuous to base an argument debunking a theory on what almost seems to be a constructed misinterpretation or misunderstanding of that theory. That, in essence is what has happened to hierarchical theory at the hands of its detractors. Unfortunately the damage has gone way beyond one group of thinkers losing an argument simply because of a facile counter argument. What has been left is an unbalanced alternative which has been instrumental in much of the social disruption that has emerged since the new millennium.

The concept of hierarchies was actually introduced in the Sixth Century by the Christian mystic Saint Dionysius the Areopagite[11]. His hierarchy referred to the nine celestial orders that were accessible depending on the depth of knowledge and virtue achieved through contemplative awareness. The top positions were occupied by Seraphim and Cherubim, while archangels and angels were down at the bottom. Naturally, the higher or more intense the contemplative awareness achieved, the further up the hierarchy. The big difference with Dionysius' model and the more prosaic interpretation of the word itself was that each successive level or hierarchy was more inclusive and encompassing of the previous level. The 'higher' did not just refer to the more advanced state of that level, but to its width or breadth in that it had taken in and included the level below it. If the level below failed, then so did the higher level. Of course, if the higher level failed then the lower level would be left intact.

Starting with the natural sciences, it is not difficult to envisage a hierarchical build up from atoms, to molecules, to cells, to organisms. These can actually be seen down to the molecular level at least and certainly upwards. In the same way, language can be seen to be made up of symbols or letters, which make words, which make sentences and as the complexity or level rises so the embracing and embodiment of the lower levels increases. Take away the symbols or letters and the language collapses. The concept of building on top of but embracing and including the lower levels is absolutely crucial to the essence of Hierarchy. Another way to look at the individual building blocks is to think of them as parts of wholes. Because things are in a state of constant change, there can be no wholes but only parts of wholes. As soon as a symbol has been devised it will not sustain itself as a whole because sooner or later it will be absorbed into a more complex arrangement whereby it is simply a part rather than a whole. So if this notion of holons is applied directly to the Four Quadrants, then those four quadrants representing the four most relevant dimensions of the Kosmos being the interior and the exterior of the individual, the 'I', and the interior and exterior of the collective, the 'we', then the whole thesis begins to take some shape.

Returning now to the Spiral of Development[12] as postulated initially by Graves and elaborated upon by Beck and Cowan and taking up the story with something of an overlap from where it was interrupted, the Blue meme embraces a collective level (LL) of psychological development which could be summarised as being the beginning of a rigid social hierarchy with immutable principles of 'right' and 'wrong'. Life now had meaning and direction, even if it was strictly controlled by puritanical authority. In the development of the human child, he is now in his early phase of appreciating that there are other points of view that may differ from his own and that he would do well to listen and adjust his thinking accordingly. Aided by education, scientific discovery and enlightenment, better global communication and greater attention being paid to humanity's well-being, the human mind and very way of thinking could advance to the next wave, Orange or in Wilber's phraseology, Formal-operational or Formop. Here the parallel advancement can be seen between UL and UR. It doesn't take much investigation to replicate these advances in the LL and LR. Once again, in order to advance from the Blue meme to the Orange meme, the higher and broader levels of thinking had to be achieved by the individual and by the collective but in doing this, the thinking and associated behaviours of the Blue meme had to be embraced, included and enhanced in keeping with the Orange and certainly not obliterated.

If the foregoing suggests an elegant overall model for the Kosmos, then why does it encourage so many detractors amongst apparently like-minded contempories? The answer is inevitably complex but it begins with the refusal to accept the fundamental concept of Hierarchy because the word is being interpreted differently. The word hierarchy has historically implied seniority, superiority, and authority amongst other features. In a school environment, there is a hierarchy associated with senior pupils and junior pupils. Because of age, length of time in the school, physical size, developed intellect or other feature, the year groups appear to be a perfect hierarchy. Likewise in a work situation, there are junior and senior members of staff, the latter who provide the management and directions for their juniors. These two examples have socially challenging consequences especially when the resulting systems enable bullying and other objectional behaviours to be justified. However, both hierarchies are the product of social development and there can be no doubt about their authenticity. As objectional as they may be to egalitarian principles, the concept of seniority by age or learning or physical maturity is undeniable. How that seniority is manifested and how it causes the senior person to behave is a different matter. Just because it is seen by some as an undesirable arrangement, it is not sufficient justification to deny it. Looking at it from a different direction, the make-up of a school or workplace demonstrates some of the fundamental principles associated with hierarchies and holons. If the members of the junior orders are seen as holons, parts of the whole that go to make up the school or workplace, then their removal ought to cause the upper levels to collapse and this is exactly what would happen as both institutions rely on the junior levels to provide the future senior levels without which neither could function. Furthermore, as the junior pupils or junior staff members advance through each organisation, by definition they reach higher levels but in doing so they embrace their learnings and skills acquired at the lower level as a part of their new level. A new meme or stage has been reached but in doing so the pupil or staff member has not only developed to a higher level but she has also broadened her outlook and the width of the new level. Without this process, neither the school nor workplace could function.

When a system or individual attains a higher hierarchical level, then by implication that is only possible because of a greater learning or the personal development of a deeper level of empathetic behaviour. If this is only achieved in part, then there is a risk of an associated pathology emerging. In a social setting this could result in the bullying and the inappropriate manipulation of the lower order. Unfortunately, this is the product of a system which is so complex, so cross-connected and interdependent on what may sometimes appear to be very obscure parallel events. There is only one solution and that is to determine the offending holon, correct its misplaced behaviour and return the holarchy affected to a balanced state. Of course, that is not always possible. The very fact that human beings move from one stage, or meme or level to the next one during their growth and development from babyhood to childhood to adolescence to adulthood is automatic cause for concern. In order to do so they must acquire certain levels of developmental thinking, analysis and resulting behaviour, but there is no gatekeeper to ensure that all the preconditions for advancement are in place with the result that many adults reach or operate in the apparently appropriate social or work peer group but they have not made the necessary advancement across all fields of development to sustain their place at that level without repercussion. Sometimes this can be dealt with, especially if the subject in question is cognisant of his or her shortcomings but where there is no acknowledgement and personal acceptance of the situation then neither guidance nor any form of treatment is possible or practicable. Only with the development of a greater sense of self and a diminution of the ego is there likely to be any change.

Many workplaces and schools suffer from bullying as a societal feature. Various techniques are used to combat this but it remains a real problem. There are two major components in action here. The first one is the level of development that the person who is bullying has achieved, or which he reverts to under any sort of stress even though he might operate at a higher level in other areas of cognitive development. And the second component is the actual society in which the events are taking place. If the hierarchy of developmental memes is re-visited, bullying behaviour is a very evident condition found in the Red meme or the Magic/mythic stage. From a societal point of view or the Lower Right quadrant, this is the age of tribal villages, and perhaps more importantly, the emergence of a human-being's ability to distinguish between herself and her tribe. In a similar way, the two-year-old child is beginning to understand more about her surroundings and is able to de-couple herself from them. The LR quadrant still has elements of the Magic level with the acknowledgement of the existence of spirits, dragons and demons but now all mixed up with powerful people who are emerging as dominant tribal figures. In feudal societies established at this stage, the Feudal chief would offer protection and care to those who were prepared to fight and work for him. There was little regard for either the nature or the consequence of actions if the objective was met. As the two-year-old develops, she may hold onto the notion of summoning up a storm every time she is deprived of something to which she feels entitled. As a small person this stage is characterised perfectly as 'the terrible twos', the age of the tantrum, but as an older member of society who has never quite risen to the next more objective and thoughtful stage of development when crossed, then there is not such an indulgent soubriquet to cover the associated behaviour. This concept of partial cognitive development as a root cause of bullying either for the bully himself or for the society in which he finds himself is still not the whole picture. There are many more contributing factors. However, when the Spiral Dynamics of Beck and Cowan are referenced, the results of their research and detailed investigation suggest that 20% of the world's population is at this level who hold 5% of the power. These are very salutary statistics.

Continuing now with the Blue meme, magic gives way to mythic. The concept of an inviolate set of principles which define 'right' and 'wrong' becomes embedded in society. If these codes and principles are followed faithfully then this will lead to appropriate reward. Society is very paternalistic with rigid hierarchies. (It should be noted that these are the domineering, exclusive and often abusive hierarchies that those detractors of Ken Wilber choose. They are completely at odds with his inclusive, higher order, greater width and depth hierarchies). There is only one correct way of thinking and of doing things. As was outlined earlier, these are the God-fearing societies of Puritan America, Dickensian England and Singapore's disciplined society established in the twentieth century. At this stage, which is also known as conventional, conformist, ethnocentric or sociocentric;[13] the growing child replaces her own limited perspective with a combination of her own and others. Sometimes this can be problematic if the child is persuaded to follow a dominant alternative, especially when exposed to strong peer pressure. She has learnt that there are her feelings, experiences and attitudes and those of her immediate group, an idea of 'me' and 'us'. However, she will invariably align with the 'us' of her peer group rather than the 'me' until she approaches and navigates her next hurdle which appears as she goes through adolescence. It's a difficult time. Making reference to Beck and Cowan again, no less than 40% of the world exist and operate at this level. In turn, they hold 30% of the power.

The next level or stage is Orange, or *Scientific Achievement.* For the first time, the individual has begun to detach herself from the 'common herd'. She is able to seek out truth for herself with the use of hypothetical deduction, experimentation, objectivity, and the advancements associated with the mechanistic scientific era. Earlier 'natural laws' from the Magic/Mythic period can be dispensed with and the new scientifically deduced replacements can be studied, elaborated upon and retained for further support. The child is now negotiating her way from the mythic through to an understanding of everything that this next wave presents. It is a most difficult transition and depends very much on her own cognitive ability, her social environment and immediate support group as to the level she achieves. This is a classic transition where failure to reach higher across all domains can lead to the development of pathologies which don't necessarily manifest themselves immediately. The leading societies of the world have become more regimented with liaisons between sovereign states, invariably to enhance value and return greater profit. It also marks the advent of colonialism. This wave aligns with the often referenced period of *Enlightenment* which not only applied to the arts and religion but also embraced the great scientific and industrial revolution beginning in the 1700s. As indicated earlier, the middle classes in Western Society and to some extent right around the world are now seeing progressive enfranchisement making a louder contribution to their environment with access to greater earning potential and all which that brings. Beck and Cowan apportion 30% of the world's population to this level with as much as 50% in power.

There is no doubt that humankind has advanced spectacularly over its time on planet earth, however, that advance has not been as a universal wave with a single front travelling across all peoples and all nations contemporaneously. This can be gleaned from the percentages that Beck and Cowan place at each level. Instead, it has grown from apparently disparate pockets of development, some on continental land masses, others on small islands. Its rate of advance has varied from place to place. In some locations it seemed to move forward at speed, only to stall and be overtaken by a different pocket. While in other places, where there was no life sustaining need for advancement, the population remained at the Beige or Purple level until they were discovered by those pockets who had been forced to advance more quickly. This was coincident with the more developed nations who were doing the discovery achieving the Orange stage complete with its associated Colonialism. The individual and societal consequences of two streams of humanity that were so far apart in their respective development, meeting for the first time and trying to assimilate one another has been huge and the ramifications remain extant to this day.

And so in the twenty-first century there is now a wide diversity of human consciousness development across the globe, which is especially disconcerting as it is most evident amongst the ruling elite. A brief look at the news covering the first six months of 2022 will indicate just how serious a problem this may yet be. Not only are there an alarming number of smaller nations with populations of less than a hundred million, but more significantly several potentially world dominating nations with populations in the hundreds of millions, which are exhibiting a very real and demonstrable pattern of behaviour from their supreme leader down through the government which is no further advanced than the Red or Blue meme. As has already been suggested, it is a common trait amongst humanity to learn to operate on a day to day basis at a level of development in keeping with 'what might be expected from a person in that position' while at the same time being trapped in and reverting to certain behaviours associated with an earlier wave of development when being challenged. The fundamental thesis would seem irrefutable. Humanity has fallen over itself with its development to such an extent that it has enabled not only the school bully to survive along with the necessary environment in which to operate but more seriously, to enable an alarming number of leaders of sovereign state governments, all of whom exhibit similar pathologies, to rise to a position of absolute authority and to remain there, sometimes against extraordinary odds.

Chapter Ten
Second-Tier Thinking

Continuing now with the concept of evolutionary advancement as represented by Spiral Dynamics, the highest level achieved by the bulk of humanity is the Green meme. This is according to Beck and Cowan's work, initially based on Clare Graves earlier thesis and then subjected to extensive additional research. This suggests that some 10% of the world's population has reached this level with 15% occupying positions of authority or power. It accords with Wilber's Vision-logic stage of personal development, in the UL quadrant. From here, the next level is Yellow, or integrative to continue with Beck and Cowan's nomenclature. To make the transition from Green to Yellow is seen as a very significant leap. The Green meme is arguably a practical plateau reached by the efforts of humankind. Some of its identifying features include the recognition of minority groups, acceptance and inclusion of alternative theories, some understanding of the interconnectivity between humanity and its environment but essentially without any spiritual dimension. While this seems to be a very promising set of features, it is riven with potential for the development of pathologies. The reason for this is that not all occupants of this level are able to conduct themselves across the broad spectrum of behaviours it encompasses. Its egalitarianism remains at odds with any sort of hierarchical theme and therefore struggles with the concept of excellence and associated value rankings. The inclusivity and desire to come to a collective solution when faced with an issue often leads to endless rounds of ineffective debate. The Four Quadrants are challenged by many of the thinkers at this level. There is a pronounced tendency to engage in reductionism by combining the UL and UR and working with the consequent mash as if it was a realisation of the whole. This has produced a very distorted view of the Kosmos, one that Wilber has called 'Flatland'[1]. It has breadth but no depth. How can the internal machinations of the individual human's psychology be represented in the observation of its external image? Wilber presented the following as an example in *Sex, Ecology and Spirituality*[2]. "I have a thought; a thought occurs to me. That's the given holon which we will use as an example. For this holon, in the Upper Right quadrant, there is a change in brain physiology, a change that can be described in completely objective terms (It-language): there was a release of norepinephrine between the neural synapses in the frontal cortex, accompanied by high amplitude beta waves…and so on. All of which is true enough and very important.

"But that is not how I experienced the thought. I will never actually experience my thought in those terms. Instead, the thought had an interesting and important meaning to me, which I may or may not share with you. And even if you know what every single atom of my brain is doing, you will never know the actual details of my thought unless I tell you. That is the Upper Left quadrant or aspect of this holon, this thought that occurred to me (And is still one of the many reasons why the Upper Left can never be reduced without remainder to the Upper Right)." He goes on to say that while it is possible to cut the body open and look at the individual body parts, such as the liver or the heart, they are only surfaces, just as the body was before it was incised. Surfaces can be seen, interiors have to be interpreted. From this simple example, it is evident that any tampering, reducing or simplifying of the four quadrants will fail to produce a true picture of hierarchical theory and the resulting reduction will be without a fundamental component of its wholeness. As will be shown, this effort to simplify something which by its very nature is inordinately complex but nonetheless explicable is both disingenuous and dangerous.

The Four Quadrants give a beautiful map of the emergence of humanity together with its inextricable linkage with every other component of the Kosmos. As Wilber has pointed out, and Habermas before him, because it was on Jurgen Habermas's, Jean Piaget's and many other notable sages and philosophical researchers that Wilber based his expanded models, the ultimate Omega Point is indeterminate[3]. Where humanity will stall remains a fundamental point of conjecture. Piaget thought that it was at formal operational thinking, which alone reaches 'equilibration' and so by itself marks the end of development[4]. This point lies somewhere between the orange and green memes. Habermas, on the other hand, thought that once a level of rational intersubjective exchange of uncoerced mutual understanding emerged then the relentless pressure was released and there would be no driver to proceed further[5]. The problem with nominating these points is that it effectively denies any further significant development. As a single holarchy that's fine, but the reality is that it is also a holon or a part of something else and therefore to stall any further development will cause a significant pressure build-up as there are many other holons beyond its own perception, and until it is able to take those larger and deeper contexts into consideration, the limitations that its stalling have prescribed will do serious damage. Looking back down below the formal operational meme or wave there is ample evidence of these pressures causing great unrest and angst.

The twenty-first century has seen the elevation of a relatively small proportion of humanity to the next level and it is here that it must abide until the internal pressures created by its own shortcomings build up a sufficient 'head of steam' to facilitate a daring and yet very important transition to a higher, wider and deeper level. It is only at this next level that humanity will begin to grasp just how much further it is possible to ascend and transcend, how much higher, deeper and wider it can go. This time, the difference between the two stages is more subtle. It does not rely on humankind making more practical discoveries, advancing the existing laws of physics, journeying beyond the earth in space flight, providing personal health care for a greater number of its citizens, adopting 'green' philosophies and practises to meet the agenda of a particularly vocal earthly group or adopting any other social reform. Instead, it relies almost exclusively on the Upper Left Quadrant, how humanity thinks. A successful transition will release all sorts of both expected and unexpected UR and LR transitions. After all, although in different Quadrants, they are all linked through sub-holons, holons and hierarchies. But what is it that needs to happen? How will it happen and when will it happen? These questions can be answered in part now because according to Beck and Cowan, 1% of the population and 5% of the power have already transitioned to the Yellow meme[6]. This is evidenced by the acknowledgement and acceptance of the concepts of natural hierarchies (Holarchies), systems and forms. A higher priority is given to flexibility in thinking, together with spontaneity and functionality. Ways have been adopted to allow the integration of differences and pluralities to merge into interdependent, natural flows. Egalitarianism is now complemented with natural degrees of ranking and excellence. Power, status and the forced acknowledgement of group sensitivities have been superseded by knowledge and competence. If this seems Utopian, then that is quite understandable. It is very much in the minority presently and typically only being championed by the normally reserved members of society who shun any sort of limelight.

The final level or meme in Beck and Cowan's work is the turquoise one or Holistic[7]. That too has an identifiable representation, 0.1% of the population and 1% of the power. To quote again from Ken Wilber's *A theory of everything*, "This is the emergence of a Universal holistic system, holons/waves of integrative energies; unites feeling with knowledge; multiple levels interwoven into one conscious system. Universal order but living in, conscious fashion, not based on external rules, (blue) or group bonds (green). A grand unification." This is second tier consciousness and is undoubtedly at the frontier of humanity's collective evolution. But even this is not the end because if it has already been achieved by some, then there is further to go. One of the problems associated with the advancement to second tier thinking is the resistance to it contained in the lower levels. The support of pluralism and relativism in the Green meme has been vigorous and overbearing to such an extent that it has almost overwhelmed the integrative and holistic thinkers. Part of this goes back to the reductionism mentioned earlier, but the main stumbling block is still the concept of holons and hierarchies which remain anathema to the detractors. It would seem that humanity has generated its own autoimmune disease.

Fortunately, the opportunity for humankind to elevate itself to second tier thinking remains extant, at least among some of its kind. But the elite group of academics, philosophers, sages and the few deeper thinking politicians will not necessarily be in the vanguard. Instead the responsibility for initiating and then prosecuting the process will fall to 'the person in the street'. And this is where the issues facing the globe today will play a prime role. While there is a modest percentage of second tier thinkers amongst those who govern, the democratic systems employed by both west and east remain firmly entrenched in the Green meme with some still clutching at those elements of the Orange, or even the Blue meme which makes them feel more comfortable. This is a sad reflection on matters, but an accurate one, nonetheless. The rise of materialism throughout the Industrial Revolution which has already been identified is a clear feature of Orange thinking and still pervades most of the societies of the world. Indeed, it is one of the fundamental drivers of capitalism on which most democracies are based. It becomes excruciatingly painful when supposedly adult forward thinking twenty-first century western sovereign state governments place the acquisition of energy resources to keep their own industries and their populations comfortable ahead of their state's basic security. There will be all sorts of eminent justification for such action, but when that security is challenged by the said trading partner's government going to war with a bordering country, the result is a mixture of incredulity and outright disbelief that such a state of affairs should eventuate. For the avoidance of doubt, this matter makes specific reference to the Russian invasion of Ukraine in February 2022 and the decision in 2012 to build a special pipeline to import huge quantities of natural gas from Russia to Germany and other European States. The idea that Europe could make itself beholden to Russia for a very significant portion of its energy needs just because it was an attractive commercial proposition shows the shallowness of thinking which remains a feature of so many democracies.

As has already been discussed, the majority of the world by percentage still lies in the Blue meme. This is a long way behind the pluralistic, multiculturism of the Green meme. It means that whatever eventuates, those who live by Blue principles and beliefs have a long way to travel to reach the Green jumping off point to the second tier. Regardless, at some stage they will need to make that transition as so many of their peers will have already done. Fortunately, there is a critical mass of 10% that is already stationed at Green. The difficulty with this is that many are still bound up in the denial of holism and hierarchy often because they are unable to break away from the more odious concepts of hierarchy associated with the Blue meme. This is a pathology that they carry with them and will have to work on if they are to be a part of the second tier transition. Hand in glove with the hierarchic antagonists thinking comes the idea of 'Flatland', that the four quadrants can be reduced to two for simplicity without losing any of the essence of the thesis. This effectively denies them any sort of access to spiritual consciousness which will further trouble their ability to grasp second tier thinking.

At this juncture, it may be helpful to tease out some ideas on exactly what is meant by spirituality or spiritual experience. If a random investigative survey was carried out on a western street, with the view to building a picture of peoples' understanding of the word or the concept implied, the responses might range from a complete blank at one end of the spectrum, to an immediate connection with any of the formal religions at the other end. In between, there may be an acknowledgement of modern day spirituality in the form of palm reading, tarot card interpretation or some perception of eastern cultural spirituality, particularly Buddhism. These answers, while seemingly quite disparate do give an indication of the steep learning curve society is facing as it tries to achieve the necessary shift but at the same time, not one of them is that wide of the mark. If the Four Quadrants approach to the Kosmos can be grasped and broadly concurred with even at a relatively elementary level, then the concept of spiritual thinking is already well established with the reader. It is the integral practice which is so important, the ability to look at humanity, its Environment, the whole Kosmos not only from without but also from within. Everything has an outside which humanity may or may not be able to see and recognise with the naked eye but just as importantly, everything has an inside or an interior which cannot be seen, only experienced or felt. By engaging with the concepts presented here, the step up to second tier thinking is well achievable. Sometimes, people arrive naturally at an understanding of spirituality as the result of a direct personal experience which may have been initiated through a formal religion or through meditative practise. Whether the subject recognises the significance of the experience is another matter. If she does then she may feel encouraged to explore the potential for herself and for others. If, on the other hand she dismisses it, then it is still not lost but it may take some time to reassert itself in her consciousness. No matter how entrenched someone feels in their thinking about another person and his behaviour, an event, the views of a particular group of people, or a piece of seemingly unreasonable legislation which prevents them from acting in a certain way, there is always another view, another side to the coin, another set of circumstances that have prevailed with someone else's thinking that needs to be considered. By pausing and reflecting on these things, the entrenched view may still prevail but it will have been tempered by some empathetic and possibly objective thinking. That is the beginning of looking at the Kosmos in a more spiritual light. Albert Einstein had a wonderful grasp of these matters, which is hardly surprising given his intellect[8]: "A human being is part of the whole called by us universe, a part limited in time and space. He experiences himself, his thoughts, and feelings as something separated from the rest, a kind of optical delusion of his consciousness. This delusion is a kind of prison for us, restricting us to our personal desires and to affection for a few persons nearest to us. Our task must be to free ourselves from this prison by widening our circle of compassion to embrace all living creatures and the whole of nature in its beauty." In this passage, there are reflections of Plato's cave, the idea of the whole Kosmos, Nature in its entirety, the short period of time that is available to human beings compared with the rest of the universe (Kosmos), and the importance for humankind to connect with its environment.

The subject will know that she can live as a member of the Yellow meme and beyond when she experiences an intensity of feeling towards another sentient being, a sense of oneness with the environment, or when she has an overwhelming experience which leaves her breathless, not because of physical exertion but because of the flooding of the consciousness with revelation. The sensitivity and empathy necessary are shown by the ability to listen to someone espousing an extreme view wildly at odds with the popular trend and not react with physical or conscious violence but instead to acknowledge that no two human beings think alike. It is the ability to feel compassion for someone who appears to have brought about his own downfall by his own thoughts, actions and behaviours. It is the ability to reserve any judgement until a complete picture of the event, which is manifesting itself becomes clearly visible, and even then to temper such judgement with compassion.

No matter how great the level of wordsmithing, spirituality will remain a difficult concept to grasp until it has been experienced and that experience recognised and acknowledged for what it is. The excitement that follows such a moment is nearly always intense and so should be as it is recognition that the next higher order of human development has been experienced. What is beyond it remains out of focus, not because of any inherent confusion but rather because of its sheer enormity. It is infinite, another word that has been bandied about for centuries with a profound absence of any real understanding. Something that is infinite is usually very big although it can also be very small. Humanity, putting aside the mythic behaviours of various religions has only managed to demonstrate its finite characteristics to date and so anyone who professes a full understanding of the infinite is probably delusional or the Dali Lama. However, there is a simple way to visualise the 'out of world' enormity of infinity. At school, children are taught that it is silly to divide one number by zero because it doesn't give any sort of answer that can be recognised. This is odd, because zero is a number and can be the answer to a wide variety of simple or complex mathematical calculations or algorithms. So why does it have to be taken away from a child's mathematical appreciation? The reason that a child is told that it is silly to try this division is because the answer is uncomfortable, it's infinity and that is a difficult concept to deal with for a teacher in a junior maths class. So, let's see whether it can be approached in a different way. Take the number five and divide by 1. The answer is 5. Now divide that same 5 by 0.5 or a half in fractions. Now the answer is 10. Do the sum again, this time dividing by 0.05 and the answer is 100. Already the answer has grown quite significantly just by reducing the number being used to make the division. So now divide the same 5 by 0.0000005 and the answer is ten million! Keep going for as long as the calculator being used will cope with the number of zeros that will appear as an answer. It will become astronomically large but it will never stop growing as long as the number being used to divide becomes smaller and smaller. But that number will never reach zero because the mathematical notation that humans have learnt allows it to be reduced in size forever without ever reaching the elusive zero simply by dividing it in half before every division into the five. And so the answer just grows and grows. It never stops because there will always be a yet smaller number to divide by. Reflecting quietly on this mathematical exercise can be very disquieting because it is so simple, it contains no tricks or manipulations but it enables a light, maybe a very weak one to illuminate an essential element of the Kosmos.

When the study of maths is taken further, the asymptote is introduced. This is a slightly less guileless way of dealing with a tricky concept! One way of describing an asymptote is by example. The fastest human being measured over a hundred metres now runs the distance in slightly under ten seconds. Over the last hundred years, the speed has improved and there has been a corresponding reduction in the time taken. If a graph was to be plotted with time taken to run the distance as the 'y' axis, the vertical one and a simple calendar stretching over a thousand years marked out on the 'x' axis, the horizontal one, then the trend of better performance and time could be shown clearly. By joining the dots representing each race recorded with a line, both historically and into the future it would appear as a gently sloping curve making its way towards the 'x' axis. As the axis itself represents zero seconds to run the race, no matter what happens, a human being in its current form could never achieve that unless the concept of time itself changes. Thus the 'x' axis can be referred to as an asymptote, a line which the plotted curve will progress towards but which it will never reach. Because it is 'beyond reasonable' to imagine someone moving a hundred metres instantaneously (Even Captain Kirk of the USS Enterprise took a few seconds to be 'beamed aboard' his ship!), the mathematical or graphical notation is not deceptive or misguided but instead simply shows the facts as humans are able to represent them at the moment. The physical world is full of these sorts of relationships. There are many results which engineers have to accept as being 'as accurate as can be reasonably expected' simply because there is no absolute answer even if the almost limitless power of computers is applied to the challenge. Bridges are designed and built on this basis, likewise pipelines carrying oil and gas all over the world both on land and under the oceans and myriad other engineered structures all rely on the 'very accurate approximations' that engineers must accept. So it is that in something that appears to be so prescribed, rigorous, regimented, factual, provable and immutable as mathematics there are many instances where a finite answer cannot be achieved. For many, this gives an almost breath-taking view of the Kosmos of which humanity, in its supposed finite state is such a significant part but for so many of the wrong reasons.

Having made much of Humanity's apparently finite limitations, by contrast its evolutionary dynamic appears to be without limit, and yet outside of any mythic or magic imaginings, there is no hard evidence to sustain this. As far as is known, human beings in their current form inhabit a finite component of the Biosphere, or physical component of the Kosmos for a relatively modest period of time. When they die, their material remains are either burnt or allowed to decompose adding to the biomass of the planet. From then on, the only evidence of their existence lies in the minds of those still living; whether through research, deep philosophical meditative practises, and rigorous investigative scientific experimentation it is possible to shed further light on this cycle remains to be seen. The capacity for spiritual connection is the biggest outstanding question. This alone is a cause for cautious optimism that there is some greater future even though all the signs in the early twenty-first century point the other way. Whether a 'Theory of Everything' can be agreed upon by a reasonable consensus of humankind is moot, principally because that consensus would seem improbable. In addition, as satisfying as it might be to the eventual authors, they will know that it will only be right for the day it's published or until some other more compelling thesis is presented. The picture will continue to spiral and evolve.

Chapter Eleven
The Perfect Storm

If humanity's progress here on earth is even broadly in line with the imagery presented in the preceding chapters then there appear to be some fundamental issues which, if left unresolved could lead to a long and painful period of practical and spiritual stagnation. The more these issues or anomalies are contemplated the more contradictory they appear to be. Homo sapiens has developed a brain which is far superior in nearly every aspect when compared with other sentient beings. Not only does it outreach and outshine other animal species in nearly every practical way but it has also developed itself to the point where spiritual communion and connectivity are much in evidence. This remarkable organ has enabled humanity to reach the staggering levels of material and scientific advancement that are enjoyed today. All this has happened in a very short timeframe. But if the routes taken and the processes used to achieve this position are examined in some detail, then much of the dramatic progress achieved seems to have taken place while most of humanity was at a lower level of advancement as defined by the Spiral Dynamics of Beck and Cowan compared with the higher levels that can be observed today. In other words, there was an almost total lack of any spiritual component driving this development. Was this a necessary process to help to build the required platforms from which to launch the assault on the next level or will it simply result in the stalling of the whole process?

Plato demonstrated a very clear understanding of human nature, both its beauty and its foibles. He was in no doubt that the most important positions in society, those that were responsible for the safety, well-being and successful functioning of a city state should be filled by those who demonstrated an enduring belief in philosophical thinking and who conducted their lives accordingly. All other members of society were flawed in such a way as to make their tenure of these positions less than ideal. In Ancient Greece, this was met with the level of contempt and dismissal that Plato predicted and there is little doubt that it would see the same reaction today if such a proposal was postulated by a western political party. It should be remembered that the State found a way of removing Socrates, Plato's early mentor from any form of political involvement by having him incarcerated and then executed. Today, someone who espoused philosophical thinking or who presented themselves as a philosopher would very likely be seen as a theorist who resided in academia, away from the hard hitting realities of daily life. She would be ill-equipped to deal with the cut and thrust of politics having been insulated from any similar environment chiefly through her studies and therefore would be given no serious political attention. Furthermore she would almost certainly be seen to be lacking the 'life experience' obtained by working in industry which is considered by many to be an essential qualification. The position today is really no different from the one nearly two and a half thousand years ago. The death sentence may not be wielded so freely by western states anymore but there is ample evidence of philosophers and great thinkers of the late twentieth century who have been ex-communicated from society by the autocratic leadership of the state in which they lived.

Plato's scenario was structured on a make-believe city parallel to the one in which he was living. It would have had all the facilities, features and conveniences that were in common usage. There would have been a clear understanding amongst the population of the nature of a government hierarchy, the need for law and order in a regimented society, the importance of establishing trade with other nearby communities, and the requirement for a supporting agricultural system and individual artisans to provide blacksmithing, cobbling, stoneware manufacture and all the other necessary accoutrements of a civilised city of the time. Plato's experimental city was to be lowered into an environment which had matured from the earliest Agrarian Age settlements some eight thousand years before. This maturity was the product of tens of thousands of hours of labour in the fields, the weathering of catastrophic losses brought about by natural and human made events, endless hours devoted to animal husbandry, countless battles with neighbouring communities, the rearing and education of children, and the investigation, mining, refining and use of naturally occurring minerals and all the myriad activities that went towards the development of Homo sapiens from hunter gatherer to city dweller.

While Plato demonstrated an extraordinary grasp of the higher reaches of a human being's mind and the existence of both practical and spiritual connectivity with its peers and its surroundings, these characteristics would not have been much in evidence eight thousand years before. For humanity to have moved from hunter gatherer to city dweller would have taken an enormous amount of sustained physical and mental effort exerted by generation after generation with little immediate reward other than simple survival. This in turn would have required a very different mindset from the one Plato was familiar with. In the early days of the new agricultural community, there would have been the need for outstanding leadership, enormous reserves of physical and mental strength, resilience to setbacks, a willingness to be a part of a pool of labour, to work in teams, to receive and discharge orders from the hierarchy that would have been essential to optimise the use of labour and to maximise the use of individual talents, to share resources, to forgo precious allocation of food in times of hardship and to offer sympathy and support to the less able members of the community. Without these features none of the communities would have survived. Not only did they survive but they thrived and developed so that small communities became bigger, the reliance on agriculture diminished as trade with other settlements began and the development of mining and manufacturing work ensued. Bricks and stone replaced timber for housing, transportation moved from walking to riding other animals, carts and other mechanical devices appeared on the scene, and those near the coast advanced the use and development of boats for transport and fishing. Humanity had taken off but so had his pathologies!

Because the Graves Spiral of Development is not linear nor does it have tidy neat edges and surfaces distinguishing one wave or level with the next, it is not immediately obvious what stages Plato's ancestors had already passed through. Certainly, they would have gone beyond Beige, the Archaic or Instinctual to Purple, the Animistic. This level would have served the establishment of their Agrarian settlements but they would have had to revert to their learnings, behaviours and survival reactions from the Beige level on many occasions in order to meet the daily challenges. By the time Plato was on the scene, the majority would have been at the Red stage or Power Gods. It should be noted here that the gods of ancient Greece were not the same as the Christian God or the Allah of Islam as they were not endowed with omnipotence. Generally speaking, they demonstrated similar behaviours as their human counterparts although rather more powerfully and they were mostly immortal. Some of

Plato's contemporaries would have been operating at the Blue level and it is here that this society would remain for nearly two thousand years.

It was Plato's opinion that the benefits and pleasures that were being enjoyed as a result of the constant pursuit of wealth, power and fame, were distorting and corrupting the very souls of the city fathers. Attachment to these indulgences said Plato, such that they became the focus of very existence caused reason to become the slave of emotion and appetite when it should have been quite the reverse, and reason should have been the master. Only in this way did humanity have a chance to keep itself well separated from its animal cousins. While these sentiments might seem somewhat old-fashioned, especially in their presentation, they are as relevant today as they were in Plato's time. Why is it that these lifestyle goals have become so important? Is it a case of 'just reward' for the enormous physical and mental effort expended in either driving or being driven from a state of subsistence farming, often little better than mere survival to the present day city state? Did humanity simply decide to 'rest on its laurels'? Or is this a sign that some sort of embedded contradiction or conflict lies within this glorious triune brain?

While the general public's perception of the philosopher might appear to be largely unchanged, this is only a very small part of the overall picture. Those people who have featured strongly in humanity's history tend to be the discoverers, the scientists, the engineers, the military leaders, the creators of great wealth or social reform, the artists, the writers, the composers, and in today's society, the entertainers. Many of these people have shown a measure of philosophical thinking or spirituality, some would argue quite at odds with their main occupation. The authors', artists' and composers' lifeworks lie close to the sensitivities of humanity and thus their association with matters philosophical and spiritual is invariably quite evident. However, for those who have gained their notoriety through scientific endeavour or through military performance, the connection is more striking. The Roman Emperor, Marcus Aurelius is a classic example. He was a noteworthy military tactician and leader and yet his 'Meditations' show his level of spiritual connection and his philosophical thinking[1]. Albert Einstein is chiefly remembered for his theory of relativity as well as a life dedicated to the study of mathematics and the physical sciences and yet his appreciation of humanity's urgent need to embrace the Kosmos and all its sentient beings is clearly evident in his words referenced in the previous chapter. Leonardo Da Vinci is applauded for his vision, artistic ability and engineering genius. To accompany these talents he had a great appreciation of humanity's purpose. There are other scientists, engineers and heroes of humanity who have demonstrated their very strong spiritual or religious beliefs but they are usually secondary to their primary skills and therefore not as publicly evident.

If the search for a parallel level of philosophical thinking is turned to the broader reaches of society and the workplace then a different picture emerges. Humanity has become extraordinarily competitive over the last three hundred years. The consumer society, materialism and capitalism have all driven this feature. The sense of entitlement that goes hand in glove with it has added yet more fuel to the fire. Life has become a competition and the winner has to be the best person. To be that best person it seems that bullying, cheating, manipulating, being economical with the truth, denigrating, practising misogyny, or in the limit, committing crime all become acceptable means to justify the end. All of these human traits are in evidence throughout history and it will be argued that they represent little more than the 'hard edge' that humanity has needed to rely on in order to make the progress it has in overcoming the odds that it has faced. Of course, there has been a parallel set of principles practised wherever possible which eschew these blatantly selfish, egotistical, aggressive and often dishonest techniques but because their drivers are far removed from the confrontational and aggressive behaviours of the majority they are considered a poor alternative, certainly not capable of delivering the rewards sought so avidly.

Have humanity's achievements been won on the back of a very different set of behaviours compared with those that the Spiral of Development suggest are unfolding today? Would the multiple waves of internecine warfare, the succession of environmental disasters, famines, plagues, and the interminable search for better, cleaner, faster, cheaper ways of discovering, manufacturing and constructing all the utilities and facilities that humankind has come to rely on only have been possible with this aggressive and confrontational mindset? When the planet is considered in its entirety without the presence of Homo sapiens it seems that it has always managed to balance itself. It has benefitted from an atmosphere that has supported natural life, both plant and animal for millions of years. There have been natural volcanic events and meteorite strikes which have had a severe short term effect, but these have been weathered and at worst have only lead to redistribution or in some cases the loss of an animal species as a consequence. However, right from the very early days of humanity's arrival on the planet there have been a string of unprecedented consequences. It began with the loss of innumerable animal species, hunted and killed for food. With the advent of the use of fire, vast tracts of natural plant growth have been wiped out. Deforestation has continued for centuries initially for the collection of building materials and later to repurpose the land for other uses. Hand in hand with the physical destruction has come pollution, gaseous, solid and liquid. This has spread across continents, through rivers, oceans and seas. Now, some 70,000 years on, the damage caused initially has been compounded by far more sophisticated attacks. On this basis can humanity honestly expect to remain welcome on the planet or has it been the master of the creation of its own perfect storm?

Chapter Twelve
Where to from Here?

The situation facing humanity today is unique. Past challenges have always been tangible whether they occurred naturally or were man-made. There was always very visible evidence, if not of the cause then of the consequence. In contrast, the evidence and consequence of Climate Change appear to be largely subjective. To point to a degree Celsius change in mean temperature for a particular area of the planet occurring over a period of 50 years lacks the drama humanity usually thrives on. To then extrapolate that change and claim that in the next 50 years, if unchecked it will rise another one or two degrees and cause all manner of problems simply fails to stimulate the necessary reaction. To then demand that there needs to be wholesale change to the most fundamental facilities that have come to be universally relied upon across the planet results in great swathes of humanity just shrugging their shoulders with incredulity. This widespread apathy is not helped by the fact that many of those who are disinclined to acknowledge the severity of the situation are in positions of considerable authority, either among sovereign state governments or at the helm of industries that are at the heart of matters. When the three billion plus souls who make up the populations of the countries living under extreme autocratic governments are added to the overall picture, the prospect of a unified worldwide response is decidedly bleak. There is a very real danger that the threat facing humanity today is simply pushed to one side and ignored because it is either too contentious, it is not understood, it is strongly refuted as little more than a political expedient to achieve some other end or it is simply too inconvenient to acknowledge and deal with. These reactions, if they are as universal as suggested, are a very sad indictment on humanity as a whole. It would be easy to capitulate at this point, recover some of the many images of dystopia that have appeared in literature over the last hundred years and simply plot a course to humanity's ultimate demise.

Fortunately that would run counter to the spirit shown during its earlier fights for survival. Admittedly, those fights were not on the scale of what is envisaged today nor were the immediate consequences so confronting. The two World Wars that were fought during the twentieth century were daunting enough, especially WWII because there was a very real prospect of a belligerent, autocratic, brutal regime assuming authority across a very wide tranche of the entire globe. Fortunately, the regime was defeated. Earlier, the developed world had been impacted by plague but its effects, although deadly were contained to a relatively modest portion of the global population. Despite their gravity and the appalling loss of life, particularly during the two wars, none of these events would have resulted in humanity's early extinction. The picture today need not be a bleak one if a global-wide initiative can be established. Just how this will be achieved remains very much in the balance.

To say that there is no consensus for taking action against the threat of Climate Change is not correct. There are a large number of national and international initiatives underway all around the globe. Noteworthy achievements in the decarbonising process are being published along with future objectives. Details of these activities have been discussed in earlier chapters. While individual enterprises and professional institutions are publishing a constant stream of activity reports, research initiatives and some future planning proposals, it is extremely difficult to assess the overall value and significance of any of this work. Without a comprehensive programme or schedule being available it is impossible to gauge the progress being made. This has to be addressed.

Firstly, the global awareness of the existential threat being created by climate change needs to be intensified with some simple, irrefutable and hard-hitting facts. This will require a consensus to be reached by a substantial majority of the leaders of the 200 plus sovereign states that make up the earth's population. So far the collective meetings that have been set up for this purpose have had mixed results. There is broad agreement that it is probably an issue but there are too many intra country complications which make it impossible for many of the delegates representing their countries to offer the sort of selfless total commitment that is essential. As was explained in earlier chapters, the highly complex interdependence between power generation, storage and distribution, industrial requirements, domestic demand, other utilities and infrastructure demand are not things that can be disassembled over-night and then rebuilt the next day. In addition, entire countries rely on the export of raw materials that support the power generation in other countries for their economic and societal survival. These contractual arrangements cannot be turned off summarily without enormous consequences to both supplier and consumer. Because of these points alone, country leaders are dragging their feet to announce anything remotely approaching total commitment to the cause. As the timing is now beyond critical, action must be taken and if it cannot be taken across the board then a compromise must be struck whereby as many countries as possible publicly declare their total unambiguous commitment. Whether this is as few as five countries or 50, it will be a beginning and they will form a vital nucleus around which others can gather. This group must be aggressive with their message and must author a simple but embracing report on the current status in all their respective countries. Each country must also produce a programme or schedule in as much detail as possible to show how they propose to achieve their targets. These schedules can be used to measure progress which will need to be made public on a regular basis. They will be the flag bearers for what must follow. Whether other countries are persuaded to engage with the same intensity is hard to judge but it will be every man, woman and child's responsibility to do as much as each one of them can as individuals to encourage their respective governments to join the crusade.

Secondly, there needs to be a rigorous worldwide training and education programme set up and put into practise. It needs to spell out the simple facts of the matter, all the issues that individual countries have to take into consideration when establishing and executing their programmes and the consequences of the various degrees of success that the world can anticipate. This needs to be an honest perspective, devoid of the typical mainstream and social media hyperbole that sadly has become the accepted norm. The teaching must be as objective and comprehensive as the Operations Manual found in the glove box of a new vehicle. It does not need to apportion blame as the blame lies in some degree with each and every citizen of the earth. It needs to reach everyone on the planet who can read; those who can't need to be taken care of by those who can. This is an imperative. Humanity has already squandered the opportunity to counter the effects of Climate Change absolutely, so now it's a case of playing 'catch-up' to minimise the consequences of what remains within its control. If the world can pull together to stamp out a pandemic then it must be able to address this with the same degree of urgency.

Thirdly, the nucleus countries must maintain a constant dialogue between themselves and be ready to include new countries as soon as they are in a position to make the critical commitment. It is essential that the whole process remains apolitical for the consequences are way beyond politics. Policies need to be trimmed and modified as progress is made or issues are tackled. They must be transferred from one government to another as new elections dictate. Although possibly an unfortunate parallel, each country is effectively at war with itself, striving to reverse the consequence of the misguided excesses of the last three hundred years and until victory has been achieved, that footing must remain. For those countries who claim that the whole process is too hard, or impossible because of their special circumstances then they must be offered help and guidance from those more fortunate. For the autocratic, dictatorial regimes of the planet, there is a limited amount that can be done short of treating them with the same contempt and brutality with which they deal with their non-compliant citizens. That is not an option for the balance of the world to adopt, especially when it is on the cusp of reaching up to the next level of human development, the beginning of the second tier. And so not all of the world will be able to comply but hopefully it will be enough to make a difference.

Fourthly, humanity needs to take a long hard look at itself. There have been countless self-help books written over the last hundred years pointing out the shortcomings of the day. There have been heart-wrenching accounts of the blacker behaviours of certain sections of the world's communities together with an evocation to 'do better'. There have been social histories criticising past behaviours and demanding accountability and sometimes retribution from the heirs and successors. Some countries have gone as far as re-writing their history to make it seemingly more palatable for today's generation. Society has turned its attention to social welfare, intervening in peoples' lives who have found difficulty with navigating life's pathways on their own. Minority groups have been embraced and their status supposedly brought into line with the majority. Society has tried to behave in a more egalitarian, pluralistic way but is this all making the sort of difference that is needed to deal with the pathologies being exposed daily as humanity evolves? To answer that question it is necessary to see just what these supposed pathologies are and where they are believed to have been generated. Only then will it be possible to suggest ways in which they can be tackled and humanity can really begin to clean itself up.

The emergence of these pathologies has already been introduced. To recap, they are based on the notion of a complete set of behaviours being associated with a particular level of human evolution. These levels are mirrored by the human child once it emerges from the womb and undertakes its own developmental growth through childhood, into adolescence and through to adulthood and maturity. The pathologies are the product of the human child's inability to grasp and apply the whole depth and breadth of each successive level associated with developing from newborn infant to adulthood. Certain behaviours which should correspond to a particular level of evolutionary development or individual growth and maturity are not evident. On closer inspection it can be seen that they are stuck at a lower level with some elements of their development. While the individual adults are seen to be conducting the bulk of their lives at one particular level, there is a clearly observable regression in certain behaviours often when a particular set of conditions prevail. To give a simple example, the inability to contain the sense of being 'wronged' while driving a motor car invariably results in the drivers taking unnecessary risks to demonstrate their annoyance and in the more severe examples, seeking retribution with physical violence, a phenomenon common enough for it to have earned its own identity, 'Road Rage'. The perpetrators may well be living their lives in the Orange meme but this sort of psychological response and consequent physical behaviour lies firmly in Blue meme or possibly, even lower. There may be countless extenuating circumstances which can 'justify' this sort of reaction but regardless, it demonstrates that the individuals concerned have not been able to develop all aspects associated with thinking and behaving at the higher level, and when put under duress regress to a more primitive response.

Sadly the very pathology that lies behind road rage is alive and well amongst those who hold powerful positions in both industry and politics. The media is forever reporting on ugly behaviour throughout both theatres. Bullying in the workplace is rife which few people in industry would deny. Hierarchies supporting and supported by autocratic management structures prevail. While ability is recognised, the developmental level at which employees operate is invariably ignored or simply not acknowledged which leaves the door open for regressive behaviours to dominate. Distressing levels of misogyny remain a feature of much of western society. Perhaps even more disturbing is the behaviour of country leaders. At this time, it is easy to point the finger at the leaders of autocratic countries who are happy to resort to physical violence to achieve the outcomes sought. When that violence is directed at their own people or at adjacent nations it causes an outpouring of outrageous indignation by those countries that consider themselves above that sort of behaviour. Unfortunately, the very countries that are invariably most vociferous in their condemnation are perfectly capable of resorting to similar tactics if the story they tell themselves and their apparently democratic populations are sufficiently convincing. It is only necessary to look back to the invasion of Iraq not long after the new millennium to demonstrate that. The spectre of 'weapons of mass destruction' was wheeled out as a justification for a wholesale onslaught of a sovereign nation by a college of 'western bullies'. The fact that this story was pure fantasy was hidden by the hyperbole of political statements backed up, on this occasion by a sycophantic and equally hyperbolic media. It seems that physical violence remains a perfectly acceptable way of righting any perceived wrongs. This is a very hard pill for many people to swallow some 77 years after the end of the Second World War, when so many nations publicly declared their intention 'to have done with war'. And yet it appears that whole supposedly sophisticated nations can find the justification to regress to actions in keeping with the Blue meme if they feel aggrieved. It is Yuval Harari's contention, identified in an earlier chapter, that Homo sapiens emerged as the dominant species of ape over the Neanderthals more than 200,000 years ago, because of its ability to tell stories. In those days, the story telling would have facilitated the discovery of the location of food, the presence of wild animals or the threat of a possible attack from another group. Eventually, this newly developed and rather original skill gave Homo sapiens an upper hand in the evolutionary struggle and the less imaginative Neanderthal began to lose its position in the hierarchy. How ironic then, that this very same ability is being used over 200,000 years later to hoodwink fellow humans into believing that 'black may well be white' and therefore the justification for mass brutality exercised over another group is entirely appropriate. The irony becomes overwhelming when this very trait leads to the eventual destruction of humanity, perhaps, in very short order, through nuclear war or over a much more protracted period of Climate Change. In both cases, stories have played a major part in either justifying outrageous action or convincing a majority that no action is really necessary.

So if it is so easy to slip back three quarters of a century with something as horrific as war, what chance is there of appealing to the higher ideals of the nations of the world over the matter of Climate Change? Today, there are two countries with nearly 200 million souls between them that are actively engaged in their own war, the larger one attacking and the smaller one, defending. In order to mount such an attack, the larger nation has had to justify its action to itself, its people and the outside world by creating a story. This story could only ever be sustained by Blue meme thinking but it is probably even more regressive than that. It is against this backdrop that the peoples of the world must now marshal themselves to overcome an even bigger foe, Climate Change, something which has become a very real threat not just to a few countries but to the whole of humankind.

Naturally when a large body of humanity is challenged it looks for leadership. Today, this comes in the form of government together with enterprise and industry. The leaders of industry are invariably the ones who have reached their material nadir. While some are firmly ensconced in the Green meme or even the Yellow Meme, the first of the two levels of integral consciousness, they invariably resort to operating at a lower level when it comes to expanding or even sustaining the empires that they have grown or are responsible for. It is these regressive behaviours which are demonstrated by industry and country leadership and emulated by management and lesser politicians respectively that are making the prospect of the necessary wholesale rejigging of both government and industry to compensate for Climate Change so very difficult. Fortunately, this situation is not true universally. There are some industry leaders and senior political figures who have grasped the nettle. Whether their efforts end up being overwhelmed by competition or governments who become less engaged because of re-election pressures, remains to be seen. Whatever the mechanism which might result in the whole process making less than adequate progress or stalling completely, it is essential to promote an alternative initiative which is not restrained by vested interest, whether political or commercial. That initiative comprises the wholesale mobilisation of the 'person in the street'. Never in the history of humankind has it been more important to speak with one voice and to pursue a course of action with unrelenting determination. Only the combined power of humanity, men, woman and children acting together throughout every country in the world will it be possible to mitigate the effects of Climate Change such that successive generations at least have a chance of being able to adapt themselves to the new environment that will envelope them.

Chapter Thirteen
The Mobilisation of 'The World Society'

It seems that most of the world's democratic leadership is either preoccupied with maintaining power for itself and whatever political party that sustains it or is forever embroiled in bickering with its opposition over internal country matters. This is to be expected as it describes a large proportion of the cycle of politics at work in democracies and despite this apparent malaise, things do happen and progress is made but often not in those areas that are perceived by others as being most pressing. And so it is entirely fitting that the urgency that some would wish to see Climate Change being addressed is not always evident. As it is clearly a very real threat to humanity's living style and possibly, over the longer term, its very existence, this has become a serious state of affairs.

In the last few months, there has been a significant international distraction. Some very focussed political rhetoric has been evidenced which has been followed up by timely action from a number of western leaders. All this has been in response to the Russian invasion of Ukraine. While the attack itself is yet another example of humanity's pitiful progress towards a higher level of evolutionary development, the reaction from other nations has been heartening. This can be seen at a number of levels. Firstly, the outrage felt by fellow democracies over such appallingly barbaric and medieval behaviour has been turned into practical support for Ukraine. While the country desperately needs physical military intervention, it has been acknowledged that there is an extremely high probability that this will simply escalate the confrontation causing far more death and destruction. There is a real possibility of that escalation reaching all the way up to a nuclear exchange which would be catastrophic. Instead, these countries have demonstrated their support with the provision of huge quantities of military equipment.

Secondly, the attack has been roundly criticised. Many world leaders have called for an immediate cessation of hostilities and a complete withdrawal of Russian troops. Thirdly, there have been significant widespread international commercial and economic restrictions placed on Russian individuals and on Russia as a nation. These include substantial targeted commercial sanctions, withdrawal from trade agreements and the wholesale isolation of Russia in its dealings with a large part of the world's economies. While none of this is specifically what Ukraine has asked for, the provision of which would have almost certainly elevated the intensity and breadth of the fighting, it has demonstrated the willingness of kindred nations to support one another and at a higher level of evolutionary development than just 'joining in the fight'. The outcome for Ukraine remains uncertain. But what it has demonstrated is that there are nations on earth who have the capacity and the willingness to operate at a higher practical and spiritual level. It has required the invasion of a sovereign state by an aggressor to initiate this response but its significance should not be underestimated.

While the daily reporting of the consequences of an all-out war can be very distressing, by contrast, they can be hugely helpful in focussing people's attention in trying to address the matter. However, the immediate results of Climate Change are nothing like so visually dramatic. The early effects are subtle, often contestable and invariably their absolute timeline is uncertain. However, the urgency is real and no amount of smart political talk will hide it as is so often the case with other issues before governments. Widespread dissatisfaction with the direction and priority of an elected government can be addressed by the voting public but it takes time because it requires considerable inertia to be built up before those who are disaffected can claim any real traction. In the worst case, it will not be possible to effect any significant change until the next election, a period of anything between three and six years. If the planet has to wait that long without seeing any tangible progress, then yet more damage will result and humanity will be faced with a more distressing end point.

A study of societal changes that have occurred throughout history will reveal that they are not achieved through violent or aggressive behaviour that invariably accompanies mass rallies or marches but rather through more subtle forms of encouragement and persuasion. Name calling, stone throwing, personal abuse, demonising and worse invariably delay any progress towards change. Erica Chenoweth[1] and Maria. J. Stephan[2], the authors of the book *Why Civil Resistance*

Works: The Strategic Logic of Nonviolent Conflict [3] offers a full account of their research conducted into the idea of such changes. "For more than a century, from 1900 to 2006, campaigns of nonviolent resistance were more than twice as effective as their violent counterparts in achieving their stated goals. By attracting impressive support from citizens, whose activism takes the form of protests, boycotts, civil disobedience, and other forms of nonviolent noncooperation, these efforts help separate regimes from their main sources of power and produce remarkable results, even in Iran, Burma, the Philippines, and the Palestinian Territories. Combining statistical analysis with case studies of specific countries and territories, Erica Chenoweth and Maria J. Stephan detail the factors enabling such campaigns to succeed and, sometimes, causing them to fail. They find that nonviolent resistance presents fewer obstacles to moral and physical involvement and commitment, and that higher levels of participation contribute to enhanced resilience, greater opportunities for tactical innovation and civic disruption (And therefore less incentive for a regime to maintain its status quo), and shifts in loyalty among opponents' erstwhile supporters, including members of the military establishment. Chenoweth and Stephan conclude that successful nonviolent resistance ushers in more durable and internally peaceful democracies, which are less likely to regress into civil war. Presenting a rich, evidentiary argument, they originally and systematically compare violent and nonviolent outcomes in different historical periods and geographical contexts, debunking the myth that violence occurs because of structural and environmental factors and that it is necessary to achieve certain political goals. Instead, the authors discover, violent insurgency is rarely justifiable on strategic grounds."[4]

While Chenoweth's and Stephan's work concentrated on the achievement of political change often within an autocratic environment, the necessary extremely complex and far-reaching changes required to embrace an adequate response to Climate Change are of similar significance and consequence, hence the appropriateness of this comparison. Women's suffrage in the United Kingdom ultimately came into being because of the extraordinary courage, nursing skills and quiet empathy shown by the women who went out to nurse injured soldiers in the Crimean War. It was Florence Nightingale and her colleagues who made such a profound impact on the thinking of the antagonists of the Suffrage movement and much less the bizarre antics of Emily Pankhurst and her followers who chained themselves to the railings of noteworthy buildings, abused politicians, and engaged in skirmishes with the police. Thus today, it is vital that the movement supporting Climate Change does not waste huge time and effort by tackling the matter using blame, name calling, aggression and worse. This will do little or less than nothing to prosecute the cause. Instead the thrust needs to be through education which will eventually lead to significant behavioural change throughout the world's many and varied societies. The youth of today in particular needs to embrace this strategy as it will be their world later this century that will reveal the consequences of their forbearers earlier inaction. The older generations can make a huge contribution to matters if they are so inclined. On the other hand, continuing to live and behave in the same way as many have conducted their lives to date will only serve to delay and degrade the final outcome. It is a simple choice but one that is not without some personal discomfort.

One of the most damaging human traits in evidence today is the ever-present desire to lay blame. It is a complex emotional reaction that has a diversity of origins. In its more elementary form it is a childish or immature way of denying responsibility for something by simply attaching it to another. In its more complex form, it is being used and manipulated to justify a consequent, often retaliatory action. The most obvious example is the fabricated stories that Russia has used to justify its invasion of Ukraine, thereby turning the blame firmly on Ukraine for the need to invade. This is both cynical and sadly regressive in terms of human behaviour. Unfortunately, it is a common modus operandi of autocratic states and can be seen in Myanmar, North Korea, China, and Russia to name but a few in the Northern hemisphere. While this is going on, the remainder of the world reacts in a variety of ways ranging from outrageous indignation to complete indifference. Of course, it is nothing short of vexatious to interfere with the internal politics of other sovereign states which is why the universal disgust being demonstrated over Russia's behaviour by many aligned and non-aligned states is, perversely so heartening. From this brief analogy, it is quite clear that the supporters of action to both deal with and mitigate the effects and consequences of Climate Change must not resort to this much sullied invective. The only way in which the concept of blame can be cited is to encompass all of humankind. Each and every member of the global human population has a degree of responsibility for the state of affairs that confronts the planet today. Some carry a huge burden, others much smaller. Regardless, there is not one soul who can claim complete innocence no matter how tiny his or her involvement. From the Chief Executive Officer of the largest fossil fuel production company to the subsistence farmer in the centre of Africa, there is no one who can claim his or her life on the planet has been without its effect on the environment. For this reason alone, it is grossly disingenuous to point the finger of blame. And when the use of blame is exposed as it has been with the Russian narrative justifying its attack on Ukraine then it is clear that such invective should be dismissed completely from the Climate Change debate. The planet Earth has a problem which has been brought about at least in some part by humankind's behaviour. By and large, those behaviours have emerged from a desire to improve the quality of life. There may not have been the necessary level of understanding of the consequences of some of this developmental action and in some cases, the justification may well have become mixed with personal greed or other less attractive human motivators, but regardless, the driving forces have their origins firmly embedded in a desire to improve the lot of humankind.

It is clear then, that one of the first words that needs to be removed from the lexicon of Climate Change is 'blame'. It is inflammatory, misleading, often completely inaccurate and most of all, unhelpful. This is a situation that humanity has found itself in, admittedly largely by its own hand, but regardless of that, the emphasis must now be all forward looking concentrating on how to recover to a sustainable position for the future. There is absolutely nothing to be gained from citing individuals, corporations, countries, governments, particular political parties or any other establishment as being responsible for the present state of affairs. It is humanity's collective responsibility for creating the situation and it can only be its responsibility to fix it.

One of the early issues which should be addressed concerns the overall level of global support or consensus that can be anticipated. This relates not only to the acceptance of the very concept of Climate Change being an inalienable truth but also the preparedness of each individual global state to commit to taking actions to mitigate the predicted consequences. There is absolutely no doubt that overall global consensus regarding the reality of the World's current position will not be reached in the near term if at all. This leads to the fear that universal action to reverse or mitigate the predicted consequences won't happen. It is because of this very issue that those countries who have accepted the reality of the situation are even more important as the initiative has fallen to them to lead by practical example. Hopefully, the inertia built up by their actions will encourage other nations to participate. While this is not an ideal way to meet the challenge, it will ensure tangible progress is made from the outset without having to wait until all nations have gathered on the start-line. The programmes that many states have embarked upon already will continue to be piecemeal and disjointed in the early stages. As work progresses, the picture will appear more integrated and connected but it will still leave those countries that for whatever reason are unable to acknowledge the reality of Climate Change firmly on the margins of the main global thrust. Any country that can tell itself a fabricated story to justify an act of gross barbarism against its own people or another sovereign state cannot be relied upon to join a universal consensus of actions and behaviours unless it suits their particular objectives. Sadly, this is a state of affairs that is extant throughout the world.

And so it is that the solution to Climate Change lies firmly in the hands of each and every person on the planet. Only by mobilising as many of the 8 billion people as possible can the predicted consequences be mitigated. This mobilisation might result in nothing more than a subsistence farmer in South America acknowledging the matter and in doing so giving greater thought to the cutting down of natural local flora when clearing land to make way for food crops. Is it necessary? Can the objective be achieved in some other way which doesn't require the proposed level of clearing? Can crops be planted which will benefit the environment in much the same way as the natural ones that are being removed? In contrast, a city dweller might consider the need to travel 'Around the corner' by mobilising her own vehicle instead taking public transport or walking. Does that same person actually need to replace the rather tired dustpan and brush she uses to sweep her porch with a new one? At the other end of the wealth ladder, does the senior manager in the London headquarters of a busy firm of Chartered Accountants need to fly himself and his family to the Canary Islands for a 'long weekend'? Could they consider an alternative less environmentally damaging holiday? The potential list of actions is hugely diverse and almost without end. The driving thought processes and consequent behaviours are common. Any proposed action, whether by individual or group, needs to be challenged to establish that it is necessary. If it is, then is this the most environmentally friendly way to perform it? If it isn't, can it be abandoned altogether or an alternative proposal adopted? In the limit, can the same objective be achieved while enhancing the environment?

All Western societies now benefit from the extraordinarily complex supply chains which deliver both material goods and food to the sale and distribution points. The choice and availability offered to shoppers is extraordinary, so much so that there is no longer any question of seasonal availability of particular fruits or vegetables. The average shopper is overwhelmed with choice whether it is exotic fruits flown half way around the world or an almost inexhaustible range of material goods, many of which are arguably of doubtful value, certainly when considering their point of manufacture and the associated transportation costs. Reducing this availability will be difficult, if not impossible. Once something has been offered to the public, it is hard to withdraw it on a matter of principle. This requires a measure of authoritarianism which would run counter to the average democracy, but is it reasonable to continue to expect this level and range of service if it can be shown that it is damaging the environment? Dilemmas such as this one will be legion in the months and years to come if Climate Change is to be tackled sensibly, objectively and effectively. Only by personal choice can the matter be solved. The person in the street has to take charge of his or her conscience in these matters. The same questions are as pertinent to foodstuffs and material purchases as they are to travel. If the demand is no longer there then the importers, distributors and points of sale will have to react accordingly and stop offering these goods for sale if their businesses are to remain profitable. This is simple 'supply and demand' at work but in the reverse direction to that which built the market in the first place. If the buyers aren't able to control the levels and types of stock offered for sale, it is doubtful that such control will be exercised by any other entity. The matter lies in the hands of John and Jane Doe.

The foregoing scenarios are just a couple of examples of where the person in the street can begin to make a difference. Of course, it should be apparent almost immediately that these simple actions are firmly rooted in a sense of empathy with the immediate environment. There are no written instructions to follow, it is more a case of how the person thinks, of whether there is the inclination or the time to review a routine task or plan from a different perspective. If the overriding sentiment is simply to do again what has been done countless times before and therefore needs no analysis, then the prospect for change is limited. But if the participants can be persuaded by their own conscience, by their peers or by media to take another look then the door is pushed open. Of course, there is another enormous benefit which could well accrue from such simple initiatives and that is the prospect of facilitating advancement to the next level in the Spiral of Development. One of the principle differences between the blue meme and the orange is the ability to view the world from a different more objective position. In the case of the child, she is now able to recognise that she has her own view of matters but that there are different views expressed by others that might be worth acknowledging and considering. It is a difficult transition but if the desire to contribute to modifying the effects of Climate Change is strong enough, this could well be a catalyst to facilitate the transition, especially for those who have been struggling to conduct their lives at a higher level and have found themselves regressing when their immediate environment seems to demand it. In other words, if the person is already operating on a day to day basis at the Orange level but still lives part of her life in the Blue meme then this could be the opening to help tackle that pathology which has been holding her back.

Where the individual may feel overwhelmed is if he is surrounded by a peer group that espouses overt resistance to the idea of Climate Change or is in complete denial. This may well be compounded by living in a country where the political party of the day is having difficulty in acknowledging or tackling the problems at a national level. For a country like Australia that has such an abundance of fossil fuels and other minerals, it is going to be a huge challenge to wean itself off the reliance it has placed on mining, consuming and exporting these treasures. This is the very essence of the country's wealth and hence the standard of living it can offer to many of its inhabitants. So how does the person in the street tackle this problem? No amount of individual empathetic behaviour towards the environment will compensate for the daily damage being done by the industries that rely directly or indirectly on these earthly riches. And this is only one end of the problem as has been shown in earlier chapters, as the mined coal in particular is being shipped overseas causing yet more release of carbon dioxide from its transport, and then burned for power generation in countries whose entire economies are built around it. The Australian government has already demonstrated its disinclination to deal with this issue which is disappointing but not surprising. The only way to encourage a reversal of this position is through an election. This has now happened and the new government has undertaken to address Climate Change as one of its election promises, unfortunately so often an oxymoron. Whether the newly elected government fares any better remains to be seen but regardless, even if it does have a more rigorous and forward thinking approach to the matter, it is only a part of the solution as the vested interests within Australia's capitalist economy will require a great deal of convincing before they agree to dismantle the infrastructure that has generated so much wealth for them. Most exploration and production companies involved in the fossil fuel industry understandably have little appetite for dismantling their wealth creating empires and replacing them with something which will lead to a reduction of the release of carbon-dioxide rather than increasing it. There is some evidence of industrial action in this particular theatre both in Australia and overseas but it remains small and largely uncharted. In order to transform this state of affairs, it is essential that everyone becomes committed to the cause, not only in Australia but in every country around the globe. This cannot be left to 'the captains of industry', to the politicians, to the civil servants, to the myriad committees and groups, it has to be embraced by the great mass of the world's population because without adequate action the globe will be a very different and far less hospitable place to live in well before today's newborns are thinking of starting their families.

Perhaps Australia has now been given the kick-start that it needed, perhaps not. Time will tell whether the newly elected government can or will want to gain any more traction with the matter of Climate Change compared with its predecessor when it comes to engaging with its fossil fuel based industry leaders. Little snippets of news immediately after the result of the election was made public suggest that the new leadership is proposing to 'do nothing' with the coal industry other than to develop it further with the release of new mining licences. This may or may not be true but regardless, it is for this very sense of uncertainty that each and every Australian needs to be engaged with a country-wide initiative to make sure that the inertia built so far around the desperate need for action is not squandered but instead is enhanced by a mass mobilisation. This does not look like the occupation of public and private land around the New Zealand government's Beehive back at the beginning of 2022 which began peacefully enough but ended with law breaking, damage to property, intimidation, and physical abuse of members of the New Zealand police force while the demonstrators tried to make their case about various matters that offended them. This is a direct hark-back to Emily Pankhurst chaining herself to the iron gates of Buckingham Palace demanding suffrage for women. It did less than nothing then and the contemporary affray in New Zealand has achieved exactly the same outcome for its participants. The mobilisation of the person in the street is first and foremost a thoughtful one. It is not, 'let's go and demonstrate and have a 'bundle' with authority!' That will do considerably more harm than good. No, this is something that has to be far more thoughtful and selfless.

Each member of humanity needs to reflect on their life and the way it is lived. There are a number of questions that they can ask themselves. Have they heard about Climate Change? Do they understand what it's about and what is at stake? If the answer to either of these questions is 'no', then they need to go and find someone who can answer both of those questions and help them to understand the main issues. This response will vary wildly from the subsistence farmer in Central Africa to the young apprentice plumber in South Australia. Both example people are equally relevant and equally important, the farmer for his interaction with his immediate environment and what he can do differently or better to minimise any negative impact on the environment through his actions and the apprentice plumber for her part in the working and social environment in which she lives. She will have a far more complex set of questions to ask herself and a similar number of responses compared with the farmer but both will play an essential part in the overall picture. One of the biggest challenges that the plumber will face will almost certainly be from her peers. Will they champion Climate Change or not? Will they belong to the dismissive group who have no inclination to acknowledge it as an issue, will they be simply misinformed or will they have some serious anxiety of their own and be keen to make a personal contribution, however modest that might be? Because of the inevitable peer pressure, the plumber's apprentice will need to be sure of herself and her views and if not, be prepared to seek advice and help from others. Provided that she is prepared to tackle these immediate distractions, and she can answer positively to the two basic questions, then she can move forward to consider other elements of her overall response. Is she happy with the way she is conducting her life? Is her selected mode of transport the best she can do for the environment? Could she change it if the answer is no? Could a change involve car-pooling with others or is she in a position to change her ICE car out for an electric vehicle in which case she may be able to consider helping her colleagues with their daily commute?

Many of the things that can be addressed are life choice matters and these may well be already set in stone and be very difficult to change without considerable cost and inconvenience. Even if the person in question is sufficiently selfless to accept the inconvenience, she may not be in a financial position to make such significant changes. In which case, it is a question of addressing those things that are possible to adjust. Meanwhile, the subsistence farmer will be struggling with the idea of crop changes. Will they suit the environment better? Can they still provide him and his family with what he needs? Compromise will be required everywhere but if everyone has an eye for 'doing whatever is in their reasonable control' then great progress can be made if enough people commit to the task. Of course, in an ideal setting, with this approach will come a sense of empathy with the environment and with each other. What is important to avoid is the concept of 'blame'. This is not about complaining and blaming someone else. It is not about having to make a change because the government of the day is not doing what it should or because the big corporations are not participating they way they should, it is simply applying individual effort in areas that are reachable to contribute to the overall progress. The demonstrable changes that John or Jane Doe can make, even in the most modest way will soon be evident. Those that contribute in this way will become the Florence Nightingales of the global response to Climate Change. This is not fanciful or idealised invective, it is thoroughly practical advice which if heeded can build to a level which will enable enormous pressure to be placed on individual governments, corporations and whole country economies.

Chapter Fourteen
Fighting the Disinformation Battle

The biggest army of private citizens the world has ever seen

The next five years are possibly the most important five years the world has seen since Homo sapiens began to populate it. Why? Simply because there must be a wholesale mobilisation of everyday people reaching every corner of the globe if the problems associated with rising atmospheric temperatures are to be addressed. There is not enough collective inertia being developed by industry and governments alone. Their efforts are piecemeal at best and are less than adequate to deliver the radical changes that must occur. Blaming the world's industrial and government 'establishments' is a negative reaction which will be counterproductive in achieving the desired outcome. The collective attention must be focused on positive behaviours simply summarised by, "What can I do?"

The various pictures painted in the previous chapters now need to be brought together. When the thread that links them all is pulled taught, it leads to a very clear and obvious conclusion. Humankind and humankind alone is completely responsible for the position it finds itself in today. While there are certainly individuals, governments and industrial corporations that are more responsible than others, the value of laying any higher level of blame on them is pointless and counterproductive. The collective response now must be directed at initiating and executing the myriad viable solutions that have been identified. Some of these are available today and can be enacted immediately. Others are in their infancy and will require prodigious effort on many peoples' parts to bring them to fruition. Just as the person in the street provided the sustaining forces to drive the Industrial Revolution by constantly applauding every new technology and enthusiastically adopting anything that would make life more tolerable and comfortable, so that same person's heirs must now champion the enormous effort required to develop new technologies and initiatives that are so necessary to meet the threat. For the last 300 years, humankind has focussed its attention on expanding and developing the engineered environment that supports the populations of the world. Now it must turn its attention to saving the good that has been created throughout those years while removing the harmful consequences which were overlooked or simply not understood. There is no 'rocket science' for John Bull or Jane Doe to master. The world's countries are blessed with an enormous pool of technical talent, much of which is already heavily committed to the cause. What is lacking is the wholesale support needed to accelerate the process and sustain it.

Today's media is full of disinformation. This may be as simple as putting a particular spin on a story in order to suit its own political leanings; it may be a case of sensationalising something that isn't sensational or it might be as blatant as publishing a set of contrived accounts of an action or event which are substantially untrue in order to make it attractive to the reader who will then be encouraged to keep buying the newspaper. It is not difficult to draw a parallel with this behaviour and Homo sapiens 200,000 years earlier when it used the very same story-telling technique to gain the upper hand over her Neanderthal cousin. Here the stories were not published in a daily newspaper or provided directly to the target reader's smart phone or computer but were simply passed by word of mouth, most probably with a large component of sign language. The stories dealt with the location of the best food sources, the presence of wild animals, the condition of the nearest waterhole or anything else which might facilitate the daily round of hunting, gathering and survival. However, when Homo sapiens realised that he could deceive his cousins leading them to believe something that wasn't true, the result was a small victory. Neanderthal would wander off in the opposite direction, fearful of a confrontation with a wild animal leaving the newly found prime fruits to be gathered by his cousin. Is the picture with today's media really any different? The object of storytelling was to improve the position of one group over another so that it might survive and enjoy a better environment as the sole occupier. While the media is not fighting for its survival in terms of staying alive, being able to gather food or keep clear of aggressive wild animals bent on their own survival in an essentially hostile environment, it is nonetheless relying on storytelling to sell its newspapers, be the leader in its chosen field and recover the consequential financial and status related rewards. Once upon a time the media might have considered the chief purpose of its life's work was to inform its followers of the facts of any situation it reported on and the better and more objectively it was seen to be doing this resulted in it maintaining its position in society. The knock-on effect of this enabled it to remain in business and continue to make money for its owners, employees and shareholders.

Over the last hundred and fifty years or so, the media has found itself growing into the position of principal public knowledge distributor. With this status, the owners and managers began to understand the immense amount of power that came with it. This placed a significant arrow in their quiver, that of it becoming a trusted 'official' purveyor of news, stories and opinions. The consequences of this development have been alarming not the least because whoever controls the media automatically has significant control of public opinion. In an autocratic state, simply taking control of the media is just another obvious extension necessary to enhance its autocratic rule. Such action allows the government to direct the spread and effectiveness of its message, whatever that may be. In a democratic state, however, these consequences have tended to lead to the media being used as a vehicle for pro or anti-government opinion which is not necessarily representative of the voting majority. In its extreme form, especially if unchecked editorially, the results can be significantly destabilising and so it has proved with the Climate Change debate. Ironically, the so called 'Information Revolution' of the late twentieth and early twenty-first centuries has led to an explosion of information being available almost instantaneously across the globe. Much of it comes from quarters other than the mainstream, fact checking is infinitely variable and extreme political and societal opinions abound. The potential for broadcasting disinformation from a seemingly reputable base has never been greater or more straightforward. Should the much regaled 'Information Revolution' really be renamed the 'Disinformation Revolution'? Has the arrival of worldwide instantaneous information distribution simply reinvigorated that less than honourable trait of Homo sapiens to tell stories, regardless of their veracity simply to gain the upper hand?

It has never been more important for humanity to strive together as a species towards a common goal. This time, it is not for personal gain, wealth, comfort, food and warmth or any of the accepted targets that have been in the collective sights over the last three hundred years whether the subject is a Kalahari Bushman or a Trader on the New York Stock Exchange, instead it is for humankind's survival. This has nothing to do with public hysteria, political expediency, a desire for personal wealth or a perverted scheme to disadvantage a parallel group of humanity in order to gain some perceived 'edge', instead it is the direct response that is essential to begin to reverse the damage that has been done by each and every mortal on the planet. There is no option for some to be 'winners' and others to be 'losers' in this game, all of humanity will lose if action is wanting. The earth will be that much warmer, the weather will be less predictable and more extreme, sea levels will rise, parts of low lying countries will be inundated, plant, insect and animal species, many of which are essential for humanity's very existence will become dangerously scarce or even extinct, staple crops which the world's population depends upon for its very survival will fail, many parts of the globe will become uninhabitable because of weather extremes and possibly the greatest consequence of all, humankind will turn on itself laying a predictable and vicious finger of blame against its fellows. This scenario is not the product of an imaginative mind having been tasked with the creation of a new film script or the story for a new dystopian novel, this is depressingly real. It is evidence based and the research behind it has been garnered by some of the world's finest minds. What is potentially even more alarming is that what has been described above is simply a mid-way point. This assumes that the mean temperature rise is contained to a number of degrees Celsius by the actions that are the subject of daily discussion. But as worldwide agreement on the timing and the actual targets is still not in place, there is the very real prospect of the deterioration of living conditions across the globe being even more severe. Modelling the future that awaits a world that shows total indifference to the consequences of Climate Change might just be the ultimate disaster movie script.

All is not lost, yet! There are tens of thousands of examples around the globe of countries, institutions, companies, universities, and individuals all pulling their weight in the daily challenge for change. News articles covering these events are in plentiful supply, especially from the specialist journals, informed podcasts, professional institutions and independent, sometimes industrial based Climate Activist organisations. What is lacking is an independent authority that is dedicated to the process of measuring overall progress in a meaningful way. It is left to the individual to scan the available reports, analyse their overall significance and form an opinion. This is not a task that can be performed easily. Instead, it requires considerable professional engineering experience and a large amount of spare time which can be devoted to the search and subsequent analysis. The net result of this situation is to leave the vast majority of both interested and disinterested parties largely in the dark on overall progress.

The United Nations Framework Convention on Climate Change, UNFCCC is the essence of a World Body attempting to drive a response to the predicted threat and consequences of Climate Change. It is most visible when it holds its annual Conferences of the Parties, COP meetings. These have been held since the mid-1990s, the more recent ones being COP 26 in Glasgow, Scotland which was delayed until the latter part of 2021 because of the Covid pandemic. COP 27 was held in Sharm El-Sheik, Egypt, in early June 2022 and COP 28 has recently concluded in Dubai, United Arab Emirates. The Conferences of the Parties, COPs provide an excellent stage for world leaders or their representatives to declare their countries' progress with Climate Change matters over the preceding year and to nominate their projected targets for the coming one. There is no doubt that global progress has been made and the value of these conferences is not disputed. However, the adherence to commitments made is another matter as is the preparedness of many sovereign nations to commit publicly to programmes which will be difficult if not impossible to implement without local political or commercial risk. There have been many examples of this coming from both large and small nations. Overall, the progress being made appears to be some way behind where the nations of the world should be if it is their intention to meet the targets that successive conferences have identified and mandated. The acknowledgement of this usually results in bickering amongst the delegates, rapid exchanges between those in attendance and their respective home government departments and some sort of compromise being thrashed out by the conference so that the appearance of a united front is maintained. While this might seem to be a rather jaundiced view of matters, unfortunately it is a realistic one. However, it does not mean that the whole process is valueless, on the contrary, for it is by this very mechanism that consensus can be reached amongst large groups, often with many attendees holding disparate opinions and ideologies. Where this process fails is in its ability to reach an acceptable consensus within a limited timeframe. The reason for this is twofold; firstly the simple fact of the hugely complex organisational mechanisms which have to be brought to bear on the matter takes up a great deal of time, and secondly, the compromises being asked of many of the delegates are often extremely difficult to contemplate, never mind to actually deliver when they are going to result in overwhelming societal upheaval, huge cost and consequent government unpopularity. It is for these reasons that the efforts being made at government level are simply not enough to ensure success without the backup of the person in the street. Because not everyone is of the same conviction, it is even more important for those who have the courage and confidence to support the push for action to ameliorate the effects of Climate Change to be making their own positive contribution.

The idea of positive, personal contribution has already been introduced. There have been significant strides made in that direction with the adoption of personal transport initiatives that don't rely on the internal combustion engine. The EV or Electric Vehicle is no longer considered an oddity by many. Instead, its advantages are being sampled and found to be very attractive. The fact that the cost of petrol has ramped up significantly recently, mainly due to other circumstances has added further weight to the argument for abandoning vehicles that depend on fossil fuels for their motive power. Provided that the financial reality of selling an old and trusted means of transport and replacing it with something new and innovative is not overwhelming, it should be a straightforward process for more wealthy societies to grasp this principle and maximise the transition. While there may be some mental anguish associated with moving away from a trusted design that has served humanity for well over a hundred years and replacing it with something considered by some to be less reliable and time-proven, this is a small price to pay in terms of the benefit that will accrue to society as a whole. Regardless of such anguish, the convenience, comfort and safety associated with owning and operating private personal transport remains the same.

However, when a change results in possible hardship, deprivation of a luxury considered by many as being no more than a daily necessity, or the complete revamp of a regular routine that has served the environment well for maybe half a century, then the picture changes quite markedly and the potential uptake is likely to be very different. It is here that the battle will be lost or won because there are many, many areas where life will become more trying and tiresome before the longer-term benefits are evident. In fact, these benefits will not accrue to all those who will need to sacrifice their comforts and daily rituals because the interval will be too long and it will be left to their children and their children's children to reap the reward. Even then, that reward will not be in a form that will replicate a return to what is taken for granted today as much of that environment is already well on its way to being lost forever. The struggle now is to ensure that the future world will at least support a tolerable environment for many, but for others this point has already come and gone.

There are myriad changes that are at various stages. These range from their initial conception to being developed, tried, tested and finally brought into daily use. This will continue for the next 20 or 30 years. It will be up to the person in the street to embrace each one and give it all the support possible. Some ideas, when they come to fruition will be less than attractive. Others will require users and consumers to 'step outside their comfort zones', especially where something well tried and tested is being replaced with something different and unfamiliar. But humankind has already proved its adaptability and provided that the motivation is there to welcome such changes, the process should flow as smoothly as the Industrial Revolution did. The big difference between then and now is that between perception and reality. In the 1700s and 1800s, consumers could see that every day inventors and industrialists were all working hard to make life more machine dependent, less physically burdensome, more pleasant. Today, consumers are going to see some fundamental components regarded as being essential elements of day to day living becoming less and less available or more and more expensive. It will appear as if it is almost a total reversal of the past. In reality this represents nothing more than weaning society off one element of its staple diet and on to another one, which initially may be more expensive and possibly less palatable but ultimately better for the planet and humankind. While this notion may seem contrary, it is simply the process that has to be undertaken in order to reach a higher level of efficiency with an alternative driver, the fuel or basic energy source. For the last 300 years, it was fine to use heat generated by combustion as the basic energy medium that could be produced by burning wood and later, fossil fuels. From that, industry was able to produce steam to turn turbines to generate electricity. In the manufacturing and chemical industries, it was the essential energy ingredient once again. If anyone questioned its safety, efficacy or potential for damaging the environment they were either unheard or overwhelmed by the enthusiasm associated with the successes being achieved. And so it was that humanity drove itself unwittingly to the position it finds itself in today.

As has already been discussed at some length, the ultimate timely removal of fossil fuels from the various processes that require energy and their replacement with environmentally friendly alternatives is fraught with difficulties. Two of these are particularly challenging. The first is simply the time it will take because of the sheer enormity of the task and the practical availability of alternatives. In countries where the dependence on fossil fuel burning is not only deeply entrenched in the current economy but more importantly, where the very development and modernisation of the country is predicated on a dramatic increase in its future usage of current energy conversion techniques, the timeline to a fossil fuel free environment is impossible to predict, always assuming it would even be entertained. For these nations to be expected to modify their current usage and then to redraw their future development plans without enormous external help is beyond reasonable. Resources and technology that other countries were able to benefit from in order to establish themselves throughout the Industrial Revolution are to be denied to these relative 'late comers'. It is little wonder that there are large gaps in the Climate Change programme.

The second difficulty is the increase in the overall cost of living that in some parts of the world will be very substantial causing great hardship. These two points alone will result in many targets around the world not being met in time. Those that are achieved will come with huge celebration but also with many conditions. Not only will the price the consumer will have to pay for their new electrical power source surge, but the availability of manufactured items which were once prolific will be scarce and the freedom to travel any distance at any time anywhere in the world without constraint will be lost. The global balance of development will be upset with poorer nations facing a longer struggle to catch up with their wealthier neighbours. Only by consensus and a worldwide agreement to share and support one another can such a huge undertaking be successful. The consensus and agreement will only be achievable if humanity is able to modify some of its more destabilising and debilitating behaviours. This can only be achieved at the individual level, in the minds of each and every human being alive today and this is where the private citizen's army comes into the picture.

There have been many references to human behaviour in the previous chapters. Some elementary philosophy has been brought into the discussion and some of the more broadly held beliefs which describe the origins and workings of the mind of Homo sapiens have been elaborated upon. There is no absolute consensus to be found on the way human beings behave but there are many themes which appear across a wide diversity of civilisation. This is not a question of which religion someone subscribes to or which political party her partner supports and votes for at election times. Nor is it a question of whether someone is wealthy or impoverished, whether he lives in a democracy, an autocracy or a dictatorship. It is simply to do with the way his mind has been able to develop and what level he has reached with that development. Of course someone's immediate peers, their family, their overall circumstances, the governmental regime they live under and a host of other extenuating circumstances will all bear and have influence on his development but ultimately it remains fundamentally within the power and control of each individual to direct and advance the development of their mind. Many people begin life with profound disadvantage in both industrialised societies and lesser developed environments. They may be the children of parents who suffered unspeakable trauma themselves during their early lives the consequences of which are invariably visited upon the children in some form or another. The material benefits of a successful society may be all around them while there is a complete absence of any spiritual dimension to accompany it. Millions upon millions of human beings are born into abject poverty and have little or no prospect of ever knowing anything different. The range of conditions and circumstances that each and every person finds herself in is enormous. It stretches from the height of indolent luxury to the very depths of depravity with every possible variant in between. Despite this and without doubt, quite miraculously, the starting point at birth and the juvenile journey to adulthood and beyond do not have to dictate the eventual outcome. Human beings are born with the ability to draw on the most extraordinary fortitude and to lift themselves clear of many seemingly overwhelming circumstances. Literature and history are full of the accounts of such lives which leave the reader breathless. But what of the tens of thousands or millions whose achievements don't come to light, but nevertheless are as spectacular in their own right? There is no doubt that the twenty-first century can boast an enormous contingent of such heroes and heroines and yet all they have done is to have been successful in managing and conducting their lives in a manner that they have felt drawn to.

And so, what is it exactly that each world citizen must do if the deleterious effects of Climate Change are to be mitigated, and in the extreme, actually reversed? The answer is extraordinarily straightforward. It requires each citizen to acknowledge that they may not have reached their level of mental development that they are capable of, reflect on what that might be and set about rectifying it. Of course, if this was a simple and immediately obvious expedient then it could be argued that it should have been identified and dealt with a long time ago, so that the world would not be facing its current crises. The difficulty in dealing with the root cause lies in its very nature. The myriad pathologies which emerge as each human being moves from one level of development to the next are largely unseen or, more particularly, unrecognised. Unless the subject is exposed to a series of tests and psychological evaluations, there is no certain way to monitor her development. In fact, tests do take place naturally in the day to day exchanges with other human beings but the outcomes are not usually witnessed and recorded by an objective observer. Because they manifest themselves simply as 'behaviours of a particular character type' and even if offensive, are merely dismissed with the comment, "Oh, he is always like that!" this leaves no opportunity to investigate and assist with correction of the underlying pathology. Where they become more obvious is when pathology causes someone to behave in a manner more in keeping with a lower level of development when she is operating on a day to day basis at a higher level. This is most evident with people who have been promoted to a management position which requires them to operate at a higher level but they have yet to reach that level across all aspects of their overall development. While they may do their best to operate at the higher level, when placed under duress they rapidly revert to known behaviours associated with a lesser level of development. Sometimes, the emergence of the pathology does not prevent the subject from reaching several levels above it but as soon as she is tested or challenged in a particular way then the behaviour associated with that pathology will become dominant and the subject will perform accordingly. This is demonstrated time and time again with the behaviour of country leaders, politicians, business leaders, team leaders, peers and colleagues and perhaps most dangerous of all, in the contributors to the media on which humankind has become so dependent.

It is fair to say that humanity as a whole has come to accept the foregoing as an unalterable state of affairs. While it is very definitely recognised by some, society seems to have spent the greater part of its effort soldiering on regardless and when pressed simply offering up justifications or excuses. Society would appear to have accepted many pathological behaviours, often simply passing them off as being 'typical character types'. Many leaders of governments, industries, private societies, schools, churches to name but a few are grudgingly accepted by their subordinates simply because of the position they hold in society. History has seen the most appalling examples of this and tragically the consequences of this are being experienced in 2022 by tens of millions of Ukrainians.

For the person in the street, the remedy is not as complex as it might appear. Much can be accomplished alone simply by reflecting on personal behaviour and deciding whether reactions to events that happen on a daily basis are reasonable. "How am I reacting to my friends, my relatives, people I meet casually or work with? If I turn the tables and listen to myself addressing me in that way, is it OK or am I being unkind, thoughtless, selfish, uncaring, unsympathetic or anything else that might seem unreasonable?" It can't always be done at the time but there will always be an opportunity to reflect on the exchange later in the day. If you find yourself wanting, then acknowledge it and try to make a point of correcting the next time a situation like that arises. This is simply the application of the 'Golden Rule' which can be expressed in modern idiom by 'Do (or say) to others only what you would find acceptable to receive (or hear) from them'. The English language is riddled with clichés and it is easy to dismiss many of the useful guides to decent behaviour that appear in literature. Some are decidedly old fashioned, don't apply to modern society any more, and have been discarded. The Golden Rule is the exception, but it is 'the baby that has been thrown out with the bathwater' and society the world over is so much the worse off because of its loss!

Discussion with those who are in close communion with one another either as friends or as relatives is another very important process to explore. This is not an opportunity for one member of a household to 'bag' another one, but instead a time for some honest reflection on how each member feels she behaves and how treatment meted out by others affects her. Any concept of blame needs to be left out of the conversation. If it finds its way in, then it's time to stop and redirect the discussion elsewhere. Blame is hugely dangerous in any relationship and its flagrant use throughout society from the lowest to the highest levels is responsible for more dissonance between groups and individuals than anything else. Things go wrong, people make mistakes, sometimes people's actions are so gross and objectionable to others that it seems impossible to do anything other than cast blame on the perpetrator. In a court of law, it is one of the main ingredients needed to initiate proceedings and where some fundamental wrong has been committed on someone by someone else then there needs to be a mechanism to deal with it. Except where the judicial system lets society down and an individual is falsely accused and punished in error, the process is a necessary one for society to maintain a semblance of order. However, the need to constantly attribute blame to someone for an action or inaction outside of a court setting is aggressive, abusive and leads to tears in the very fabric of society which causes enormous unease, unhappiness and results in extensive disruption.

The 'blame response' so common throughout human society begins to emerge in early childhood, in particular with 'the terrible twos'. There are many highly readable books and articles readily available that will expand on this human trait. In *Beck and Cowan's Spiral Dynamics* as elaborated upon by Ken Wilber[1], the human child's progress through the red meme is marked, amongst other things, by his discovery of the use of blame to redirect attention towards his sister or brother when faced with being challenged for something bad he has done. As he grows and his mind develops, he advances to the blue meme where he begins to appreciate the world not only through his own eyes but those of others. This should be the time that he learns that the use of blame to deflect attention elsewhere is not always a good response and should be thought about very carefully. This might seem unreasonable to the reader to expect a child to have developed a moral compass at a relatively early age, but there are many children that achieve this. Those that don't simply end up carrying it with them as a pathology which they may or may not deal with as they grow and mature. Much will depend on their environment and immediate circle of friends and relatives. As this particular pathology develops at a very early stage it is not difficult to see how challenging it is to have to deal with it in later life if it has not been identified and corrected during childhood. Of course, there are degrees of intensity as far as the manifestation of pathologies is concerned and so it is not unreasonable to find elements of pathologies in a very large proportion of humanity. What causes such social disruption and grief are those that are so entrenched in people's daily behaviour that they define their very characters.

It is naïve in the extreme to imagine that a few simple paragraphs in a book is all that is necessary to redirect humanity onto a different behavioural path but there is not really a great deal more to be said. Of course there is an inexhaustible supply of written material that covers the shortcomings of humanity, many including the recommended methods and techniques for dealing with them. Much of this is worth consulting, but unless there is a personal desire to do so it is arguable that it is not necessary because the essence of what is required is simple. Humanity has to start behaving itself. Those quiet almost inaudible voices in the back of your head that pop up now and again remonstrating with you for something you've just done or said, either of which may be inappropriate, are the possible residue of earlier childhood behaviour patterns that you knew to be right but which no longer seem to apply in the adult world. This, after all, is the essence of a pathology which so many of us, if not all of us carry at some level. It is not difficult to justify what we do and say, after all the human mind is constantly 'chattering to itself', reassuring itself that what's just been done is excusable or justifiable or complaining that it has just been bullied, abused, overlooked or demeaned in some way. It's not always possible to react at the time but reflection later in the day can be very helpful. Most of humanity has had an idea of how to behave respectfully and empathetically towards others at some time during their development. Whether it was submerged by the necessity of surviving in a hostile environment or he or she was surrounded by equally developmentally challenged peers and adults is moot. Either way the net result is the same, the spiral of development has been stunted or if it has continued then it has done so while carrying with it a variety of pathologies which emerge whenever the environment provides cause. In extreme cases, understanding and overcoming these pathologies needs professional help. In less severe situations it is something that can be achieved alone or with the guidance of friends or family.

Earlier in Chapter ten, there was a discussion on the question of aspiring to and reaching the 'Second Tier' in the Spiral of Development. As with all transitions from one level to the next, it is a compelling target, not only because it is there and has been recognised but because it has been reached by a proportion of humanity already, according to Beck and Cowan, some 1%. More importantly, it means that those who have achieved this level of development are now operating in the yellow meme where they can begin to grasp just how much further it is possible for humanity to ascend and transcend, how much higher, deeper and wider it can go. This transition is not about practical human achievements in terms of a greater understanding of physics or success with interplanetary travel but rather it is centred on the greater understanding of the Upper Left Quadrant in Wilber's model. This time, the difference between the two stages is more subtle. A successful transition will release all sorts of both expected and unexpected Upper Right and Lower Right transitions. After all, although in different Quadrants, they are all linked through sub-holons, holons and hierarchies. With the transition there is evidence of the acknowledgement and acceptance of the concepts of natural hierarchies (holarchies), systems and forms. A higher priority is given to flexibility in thinking, together with spontaneity and functionality. Ways have been adopted to allow the integration of differences and pluralities to merge into interdependent, natural flows. This means that the Egalitarianism of the green meme is now being complemented with natural degrees of ranking and excellence. Power, status and the forced acknowledgement of group sensitivities have been superseded by knowledge and competence. This is really just a way of saying that those members of humanity that are now able to operate at this level are doing so unincumbered by the more rigorous and less flexible thinking practises of the green meme.

For anyone operating at a level lower than green, this will seem a far cry but the principles that second tier operation embody should be possible to glimpse. Anyone can begin the process of giving free rein to their thoughts, by pondering their actions and reactions to the day just over. There is no magic associated with this, no need to have studied anywhere outside the school of life. Each and every mortal has it in them to ascend and transcend as high and as broadly as they desire, all it takes is time and honest reflection. The higher humanity as a whole can climb the 'Spiral of Development' the greater the prospects are for its survival in a recognisable state.

The wide spread of human development has already been discussed in some detail. It is suggested that the bulk of humanity, some 70%, is operating in either the orange or blue memes. This doesn't mean that all their actions, thoughts and behaviours are confined to these levels as the whole model is quite fluid as has been shown. Many people who are predominantly of one of these memes are perfectly capable of demonstrating behaviours and thought processes both above and below their nominal positions. In the latter case, this is the essence of the pathologies that have dogged humankind's progress for thousands of years. However, in the former case where people are reaching beyond their nominal level, then this is cause for great celebration as it is demonstrating the innate desire present across humankind to look to bettering itself both collectively and individually. This is why, when presented with the opportunity of committing to help in whatever way seems both appropriate and possible in the fight to counter Climate Change, there is a real prospect of each and every person being able to make a tangible and worthwhile contribution. For those living in a modern, democratic western society there are many more opportunities for practical help than those who inhabit less developed societies or who are burdened with autocratic or dictatorial country leadership. Sadly, these groups make up a substantial proportion of earth's inhabitants and they may struggle to have much practical input. However, this does not stop them from contributing both spiritually and philosophically. The more people who are able to observe, reflect upon and modify their own behaviours which are the product of their interaction with their fellows, the better chance humankind has for a bigger and more far-reaching clean-up of its pathologies. This will lead to a more cohesive and integrated society which will be able to offer empathy in place of blame, sympathetic understanding of the other person's view instead of contempt, and objective, rational thinking in place of dogma. While this may seem mildly utopian, it is a state of affairs which already exists in pockets of many societies worldwide. All it requires is a critical mass for it to begin to be adopted far more widely across the globe.

Meanwhile, those living in a modern western democracy have many more practical opportunities to join the Climate Change crusade. For them, first and foremost, there is the hugely effective power contained in the freedom of speech. The general populace will not be marginalised, brutalised and eventually imprisoned for speaking out against the government or any large bureaucratic establishment. Obviously, the historical learnings of effective mass rallies and public representations are very important. Aggression and blame will do little or nothing to prosecute a cause but the peaceful assembly of like-minded people can be used to great effect. It is here that the liberated members of the world society can take a leaf out of the quiet and thoughtful behaviours of those who do not enjoy such freedom but can nonetheless be an effective force for change.

Away from the public demonstrations, there are the practical opportunities open to these areas of the world. The support for and adoption of electric vehicles is a topic already discussed. The willingness to change out fossil fuel driven home heating and cooking systems is another practical area open to many. Then there are the more subtle behaviours that need to be taken up across all communities. These can be summarised by a number of simple questions: 'Is my proposed journey by private car really necessary?' Is there a way I could share the journey with someone else to save the burning of unnecessary fuel in two separate vehicles?' Is it possible that I could make the journey by public transport?' Could I travel by bike or could I walk?' Initiatives which have been taken up in response to these questions have led to car-pooling for trips to and from home to work, people working from home for some of the working week and a significant increase in bicycle sales. While these responses are encouraging, they are simply not enough on their own and with the current levels of adoption. There has to be a much greater commitment across multiple communities before these sorts of actions will make a tangible difference. What should not be overlooked is the mindset that is required to follow these simple few examples. Even if people are not in a position to contribute practically there is nothing to stop them supporting vigorously those who can. The single biggest and most effective question that each and every adult human being must become used to challenging itself with is 'What can I do to help?'

After the capture of Iraq's Sadam Hussein, in 2004 hostilities were supposed to be over. As it turned out, they were really only just beginning and any individual or organisation that had agreed to assist with the rebuilding of destroyed or capital-starved infrastructure found themselves operating in a very hostile environment. For members of the Coalition's military forces this was familiar territory, but for the thousands of civilian contractors who had been assembled to assist with the work, this was a very unfamiliar environment. With the ever-present threat of Improvised Explosive Devices (IEDs) secreted along many of the arterial roads, armed militia attacks, often with rocket propelled grenades (RPGs) and suicide bombers either on foot presenting themselves amongst a public gathering or in a car driven at high speed across the forecourt of a hotel or public place, travel was fraught with deadly danger. However, travel was essential to execute the work which was in turn essential to improve the lot of the Iraqis after Sadam's demise. Over time, civilian contractors became used to carrying out risk analyses on any travel that might bring them or their subcontractors into danger. Always, the first question that needed to be satisfied was "Is my travel 'mission critical'?" In other words, if the journey is not made will the overall mission suffer in a way that it cannot recover from. These were quite logical and obvious analyses to carry out simply because the consequence of not making the right decision either resulted in possible injury or death on the one hand or on slowing down or stopping the humanitarian work that had been agreed to on the other hand. There were potentially negative consequences whatever the decision. The significance of the thought processes that need to be applied to day to day living in the face of Climate Change are very similar to those that faced the Iraqi civilian contractors on a daily basis, except that the consequences of doing nothing or making a wrong decision would manifest themselves quickly and sometimes, dramatically. This highlights the difficulty of adapting a familiar lifestyle in the face of a threat which is not immediately observable. The consequences of doing nothing or even actually opposing the very concept of Climate Change will not be obvious immediately as would have been the case in Iraq with having to deal with the aftermath of a suicide bomber or an RPG attack on a vehicle carrying work colleagues, but they will still be there. The difference is simply one of timing and possibly of those that will be most directly affected. It will not be the peers of those who show apathy, disinterest or complete denial, but it will almost certainly be their children and their children's children who will have to face the Climate Change equivalent of a suicide bomber or an RPG attack. Make no mistake, the analogy is ugly but it is equally real.

Chapter Fifteen
The Transformation of the Materialistic Society

Historically, humanity has been faced with enormous challenges. These have included war, plague and natural phenomena such as volcanic activity, earthquakes and tidal waves. For those that were immediately affected, there was never any reason to challenge the substance or veracity of the event and its immediate personal consequences because it was happening right in front of them. With plagues, people were falling ill and dying in public, their bodies often left in the street until the hand propelled carts completed their daily round of corpse collection. People may have struggled to understand the potential extent of the disease and to have comprehended their own level of personal risk, but there would have been little appetite for full scale denial. In the same way, when Krakatoa exploded in the 1800s in the Far East, those close enough would have felt it, seen it, smelt it and witnessed the fallout from the resulting huge ash clouds. Those further afield would have only had reports and stories by others to inform them but again, denial would have been low on the order of consequent global reaction. The two World Wars, by very definition involved the whole globe. While not all sovereign states and countries had direct experience, it would have been difficult to deny the risks and consequences of such events. Again, some observers would have elected to minimise the significance as neither event involved them directly, but the consequences would have been felt in relatively short order.

By contrast, Climate Change and its consequences to many remain matters for conjecture because the supposed results are either not immediately obvious or if they are then they can be dismissed because their connection with Global Warming is seen as being tenuous at best. Ironically, Russia's invasion of Ukraine which began in February 2022 has been termed 'a special military operation' by the Russian leadership thereby completely misleading the greater Russian population. The fact that the remainder of the world is witnessing a full scale military onslaught by Russia on Ukraine has been withheld from the Russian public and a comprehensive smoke screen has been created to hide the reality of the situation. So, not only is humanity struggling in its response to Climate Change simply because it is difficult to convince people of the reality of something as complex, but at the same time hundreds of millions of Russians and their immediate allies are being deliberately deceived by the Russian leadership in order to 'control reality' to suit its own agenda. It is no wonder that many people continue to be less than convinced about the significance and reality of Climate Change.

For those that require no further convincing, the task ahead is enormous. It will call on all the historical resilience and positivity that humanity has demonstrated in the past if the challenge is to be met successfully, and as has been shown, it will be made that much more difficult because there is little evidence to justify the significant hardships that will accompany any response. There will be no immediate death and destruction that can be pointed to in order to galvanise the necessary public reaction. Instead, humanity must accept the wisdom and guidance of its leaders as difficult as that might be now the world has witnessed such gross and wholesale deceit by the Russian leadership.

While much of the motivation for responding to Climate Change at an individual level must come from within, this is not an impossible task. It has been done before in times of national or international disaster and it can be done again. The situation has come about because of humanity's abuse of its natural habitat. That abuse had its origins in a desire to make life more comfortable, safer, less arduous and more enjoyable to name some of the more honourable motives. Of course, the other side of coin meant that any progress would arrive hand in glove with wealth for the main orchestrators. The parallel motivations were seldom at loggerheads as one simply served the other. The challenge arose because the ultimate consequence of all of this was not foreseen until relatively recently, in the last fifty years and worse still, not acted upon until the last ten. And so it is that humanity must now lean on the relative position it has achieved in the Spiral of Development. If it can call on a measure of spiritual connection with Nature and its own fellows then this will be a huge advantage. If it has yet to reach these levels of development then the daily reflections that have been discussed will be enormously helpful. It's not an impossible task, just one that presents considerable challenges.

The greatest need is for people to develop some level of communion with their environment including their peers. This is not a battle of individuals against Global Warming but rather one of groups helping each other to meet a common challenge. The idea of sharing has already been highlighted, particularly when it comes to the use of private vehicles by single operators. Common destinations from distant communities make these options very attractive. Not only will the journeys be cheaper for the individual, but they will consume less power, whether it is via an EV or an ICE powered vehicle. The uptake of these behaviours requires a measure of sacrifice in terms of independence, but this is a small price to pay for a potentially large gain. Of course, where more use can be made of mass transit systems for moving large volumes of people from one place to another, then the savings are that much greater. There is an onus on local and national governments throughout the World to prosecute wholesale improvement of these systems not only to reduce or remove their volumes of carbon released but also to make them more useful and effective for the communities they serve.

Western societies have all fallen into the trap of 'materialism'. This was largely a consequence of the Industrial Revolution. The ownership of 'stuff' became a symbol of individual success. Two hundred years ago it might have been the newly manufactured labour-saving coal scuttle which the local sheet metal works had recently commissioned, or the latest range of porcelain china which had emerged from the British Midlands. A hundred and fifty years later, aspirations would have risen significantly and a middle income family would be focussing on buying the latest model family car produced by the Ford Motor Company. Of course, the purchase would have been made over a period of time and the new owner would pay a hefty premium on the basic cost to cover the associated loan. This was the heyday of 'Hire Purchase', a simple way to make material acquisitions more available. Such arrangements continue to this day, but immediately after the Second World War they were something of a novelty and ideal for fostering a healthy materialistic society. The middle income family is now in a position to change out their car for an EV. Many Western Governments are encouraging this with the offer of tax relief or even capital contributions to help with the purchase. The future use of the ICE will be severely curtailed if not actually banned in some countries early in the next decade. Hopefully the take-up of EVs will become widespread throughout the Western World and at a faster rate than is currently envisaged. But as has already been addressed, the greatest pollution is coming from power generation and while the changeover to less or non-polluting alternatives is in the hands of government and 'big business', the person in the street can still play its part for she is the domestic end user. To begin with, there is always something to be gained from being more economical with the use of power. "Do I need to have my heating set so high?", "Can I wear a jumper in doors in the winter instead of running my house at 'shirt-sleeve' temperature?", "Can I run the heating for shorter periods?", "Do I need so many lights burning all the time or can I be more abstemious?" These are the very simple day to day opportunities to cut down on energy consumption. If just a handful of people adopt such patterns of behaviour, each according to their own circumstances, it will make little overall difference, but if ten million rise to the occasion then the country's overall power usage and consequent pollution will be reduced significantly, and yet all it has taken is a change in mindset from 'I'm turning my heating on/up because its mine and no one is going to tell me what to do' to 'I'm cold so I need to turn the thermostat up, but maybe there's another way which I can solve my problem which will be more friendly and considerate to others'. These examples may seem trivial but if there is a serious up-take it will lead to a positive change in people's thinking processes and therefore in their overall behaviours. It should be remembered that there is a parallel objective here and that is to help as many people as possible elevate themselves to the next level of development, whatever that may be. Caring how personal behaviour might impact another person or group of people is certainly a mark of being able to operate at a higher level.

Meanwhile, at a more radical level, there is the question of the type of heating a home is using. Gas, solid fuel or oil-fired central heating boilers are emitting carbon dioxide whenever they are running. "Do I have the money to change to a more environmentally friendly heating source?" This would certainly apply to those who had the resources to effect such a change on their own and should be encouraged. Obviously, the wholesale change-out of every householder's carbon emitting utilities is a longer term objective but this will require a higher level of commitment across a broader range of stakeholders. Improvements can certainly be made with new homes and the constant upgrading of existing ones. Here the market must play a bigger more practical role in terms of what is can offer the consumer. Governments should already be participating in this process ensuring that those responsible for new buildings or upgrades are directed to use only environmentally friendly utility equipment. Such measures should be embraced by the consumer as a part of his contribution. In the same way as heating systems can be targeted, so can those that cool. There is not a lot of choice in the energy source that runs them and so there is no opportunity to shift to a more emission friendly medium, but the same level of personal consideration can be given to their use and operation thereby reducing the overall demand on the electricity supply.

One of the significant components of today's society that remains firmly in the hands of the consumer is the amount and quantity of 'detritus' that is purchased daily. Detritus refers to the plethora of every conceivable gadget, labour-saving device, unnecessary and poor quality garden or garage tool, latest design in poor quality garden furniture, fire pit, unnecessarily over-sized barbeque, or innovative plastic item that is based on something more expensive but because of the design modification necessary to make it cheaper it is rendered 'worse than useless' because it is no longer strong enough to perform the job at hand. The sheer volume of items that fall under this general heading is staggering. 60 years ago, the average town of 20 or 30,000 people usually catered for the provision of practical material household items with a retail outlet or shop called an 'Ironmongers'. This was the shop where the public could buy everything from a woodscrew to toilet plumbing fittings, adhesives, carpet tacks, lengths of various steel sections, camping stoves, the list was endless. To a young child intent on emulating the practical skills of his older relatives or peers the place was an Aladdin's cave. The shopkeeper and the staff were all knowledgeable in their respective fields, be it painting, adhesives, mechanical fittings or whatever else was sold there. Long after the end of the Second World War, life for many Western countries was still austere. Resources were limited and the sentiments resulting from the profound shortage of raw materials and finished manufactured products during the war were still much in evidence. If something broke then there was usually someone who would be ready and willing to repair it. Washers were still sold to patch holes in galvanised steel buckets or in the base of a kettle designed to boil water on a gas stove. Humanity was definitely not overwhelmed with the plethora of manufactured items that are available sixty years later through illustrious outlets such as Bunnings, B and Q or Walmart. Toy/sports shops were another notable indicator of the times. To begin with, there weren't many of them. Secondly, they had limited stock. A young boy saving his pocket money to buy that particular penknife he had been coveting for months was forever anxious during the whole process as to whether it would still be in the shop when he reached his target savings. Today, the shops catering for such goods are legion and the stock is positively falling off the shelves. The population of the consumer-world is not so very different today and yet its citizens are now absolutely overwhelmed, drowned with a seemingly limitless supply of everything a human being might fancy. What happened in those sixty years?

Probably the biggest change was the emergence of manufacturing to an acceptable standard in countries outside Europe. The early days of production from Hong Kong, which was infinitely cheaper than Europe, heralded an influx of cheap, poorly made articles, often referred to as 'tat'. Initially, the up-take was poor, the quality and type of goods on offer being the main stumbling block. Eventually, the East raised its game and began to produce copies of Western goods at a fraction of the price, firstly because labour rates were dramatically lower than those of the West and secondly because of the sheer volume of goods produced. Again, up-take was initially slow in the West but eventually the East assumed control. Today, it is difficult to find an item stocked by any of the big stores mentioned earlier or any of the outlets trading 'on-line' that has not been manufactured in China. Not only has the West lost its market to the East but the volume of dubious quality manufactured items flooding the retail sector is simply staggering. The loss of the West's worldwide market for manufactured goods is one thing which brings with it all manner of consequences, but the subsequent flooding of that same market with much cheaper copies of the same products has had a far greater effect. A casual stroll around any of the larger retail outlets in the West reveals a mind-numbing quantity and choice of stock. Many of the items on display, while maintaining a semblance of reasonable quality are pitifully inadequate for the job for which they were intended. Whether it is a ceramic tile cutter which is supposedly designed to cut tiles of between four and eight millimetres in thickness or a heavy duty work vest, presumably intended to sustain the rigours of outdoor manual work, neither article is fit for purpose. The tile cutter will not cut anything greater than three millimetres thickness and the work vest loses its shape and colour after two washes. Both items are relatively inexpensive but neither will provide the end user with any practical value. The store in question continues to stock the items while the public, somewhat inexplicably maintains its faith in them and continues to patronise it. Where do these items end up? Are they simply taken home, put on the shelf for a 'do-it-yourself' job to be tackled sometime in the future or used once, found to be wanting and put on that same shelf? These are just two very simple but actual examples of the huge quantity of almost worthless items which have been manufactured in China, brought to the West by sea or even air transport, stocked by a major outlet and purchased only to be discarded. As a final and ultimate insult, the one-time use or unused products find its way to landfill rather than being recycled! This is nothing short of a tragic cycle. The items themselves require raw material which may begin its life as iron ore, mined from the ground with the associated carbon footprint, turned into steel with the additional use of carbon emitting plant, transported half way across the world in a fossil fuel burning ship, transferred from the dock to the retail outlet by a fossil fuel burning truck and stocked on the shelf of the store which is heated or cooled by fossil fuel burning electrical generation. It is then purchased, used once, possibly, and discarded to landfill. That is part of the story of the tile cutter. The work vest is manufactured from synthetic material which begins its life as oil extracted from the ground either onshore or offshore, buried deep below the seabed. The cost and complexity associated with its extraction is only matched by the amount of atmospheric pollution which results from its subsequent refining in a dedicated chemical plant and transformation into a synthetic thread. This is machined into a garment in another facility which consumes its share of electricity, invariably produced by burning fossil fuels. The transportation all the way from China to the retail store follows a similar route as the previous example and it shares its ultimate destination, landfill. This is not constructed melodrama but a factual account of just two items out of simply millions like it. Of course, not all of the stock for sale in these gargantuan retail outlets that have become the norm for Western society is useless. A reasonable amount goes through an acceptable 'whole of life cycle' but the sheer quality of much of what is sold suggests that that cycle is heavily weighted in favour of the original manufacturer, the transportation company and the retailer rather than the ultimate user and most importantly of all, the planet earth!

So what can be done? How does the West and the rest of the world reverse this appalling cycle of raw material mining, manufacturing, shipping, stocking and selling of a staggering array of next to useless articles? Again, the answer is not complex. Just as with the proposed car journey, it only requires the shopper to pose a simple series of questions and answer them truthfully with the appropriate level of compassion and sensitivity for himself, his fellow human beings and the environment that sustains him. 'Do I need this article?' If the answer is 'yes', then 'do I need to own it?'. In other words 'Do I have enough work to justify owning it or could I borrow it from a colleague or hire it for the job I have in mind?' Straight away the much sought after but so short-lived gratification high that comes with buying or acquiring something material has been blunted. Now, the shopper can assess his potential choices and if he finds that there is eminent justification to go ahead then that's a perfectly acceptable conclusion. But if this pause and assessment of his potential action leads to a decision not to go ahead because he has settled on another less costly solution to solve his problem and one that is more friendly to his pocket, the environment and his peers then that is a win for the planet. This is not fantasy or some sort of effort to pervert the freedom of the person in the street, it is instead an honest way of approaching something as simple as buying an article that is not really needed, thereby saving that sometimes huge 'whole of life' energy cost. Yes, someone else might come along and buy the subject article instead, but she too should be going through the same process in her mind before making the purchase.

For this scenario to have an effect on Climate Change it must be played out hundreds of millions of times all over the world. The immediate and tangible consequence of the initiative will be a drop in sales which will have an alarming consequence for the retail business. This cannot be helped as the trade is very much a part of the abuse of the planet in terms of gratuitous use and squandering of precious raw materials and the unnecessary consumption of fossil fuels to provide power for the associated industries. It will take time and it will take serious resolve by the person in the street. Hopefully, the industries that will be affected along with their management and employees will be able to turn their hands to more empathetic work as far as the planet and humankind's future is concerned. The other side of this initiative is the very positive effect that its uptake will have on humanity. The constant quest to own more 'stuff' and to expand the range and volume of material possessions is a sad trait of human society, particularly in the more socially and technically advanced nations. It is also something which developing nations will continue to aspire to in their effort to emulate those communities and states that have advanced further. Nothing will change unless humanity can teach itself to do without the instant but very transitory gratification that shopping and material ownership provides. The solution is there for all to see and lies simply in each and every one of us making a determined effort to seek out and advance to the next level on the Spiral of Development. And if it is not immediately possible to transition completely from one meme to the next then there is nothing to stop a partial elevation as long as it encompasses the bulk of the thought processes and behaviours associated with the higher level. There are many members of human society that operate across a number of levels as has been highlighted. Sadly this is usually the product of being unable to cope with the more spiritually challenging behaviours of the higher level which results in a behavioural regression to the lower level, a condition repeatedly referenced as a pathology. The attainment of a higher level of development will allow these adjustments that are being described to be made a great deal more easily. The question and answer sessions in front of a piece of kitchen equipment, an article of new clothing or any other material acquisition will become more automatic, less stressful and more fulfilling. To be able to walk away from an urge which is invariably only temporary but always costly to succumb to will end up producing its own 'high'.

There are many underprivileged societies and whole countries around the world that have few or none of the trappings associated with western materialism. Hugh Van Cuylenburg's book *The Resilience Project*[1] draws on the behaviour of one student in particular who was within the group of children that he taught in the far North of India. His name was 'Stanzin'. The happiness and enjoyment that this young boy found in the simplest things surrounding him, be they a pair of shoes, a bowl of rice at mealtimes or the opportunity to play on a partially derelict climbing frame and swing assembly had a profound effect on the author. This simple view of life which was accompanied by a warmth and profound interest in the well-being of his young contemporaries was something that Cuylenburg took away with him back to Australia where it established itself as the very essence of his subsequent teachings. Human beings are extraordinarily resilient. Sadly that resilience is often deeply submerged beneath an unhappy childhood which, while often being surrounded by the material trappings of Western Society, fails completely to offer any opportunity for spiritual development. Cuylenburg's time in India gave him the insight to identify the crucial elements of Australian society that are so often absent, Gratitude, Empathy and Mindfulness. It is at this level that humanity as individuals can have the most dramatic effect on the global response to Climate Change. None of it is 'Rocket Science'. That is reserved for the scientists and engineers who are guiding the world away from its dependence on fossil fuels in every walk of life. For John and Jane Doe it is simply a case of discovering their inner selves where empathy and sensitivity towards their environment and towards those that they share it with lies. Once discovered, it only needs to be practised without condition.

Erica Chenoworth and Maria Stephan's work identified earlier champions the idea that it takes just 3.5% of a community or society wanting to make change to effect that change. It is based on the study of several hundred peaceful and non-peaceful protests over the last hundred years which have brought about successful change of regime or government. The dynamics are complex and the emphasis is on determining which is more successful, peaceful or violent demonstration. The former wins emphatically. With Climate Change, the model is more complicated because the target resisting change is not just an elected or autocratic government but society as a whole. It encompasses government, private industry, public utilities, transport, air and sea travel and biggest of all, each and every member of the world's population. It is probably unsafe to champion these figures as targets for initiating the change simply because of this. However, just because the absolute percentages may not be relevant, what is valuable to draw from this is the difference between violent and non-violent demonstration. So far, Climate Change rallies have, by and large, been peaceful. There is a tendency to align them with the 'Green' political movement which is possibly disadvantageous. Because 'Green' political parties are often regarded as being on the fringes of mainline politics, this can be rather a hindrance to the cause. While their philosophical base is certainly sound in part, the popular view of the party's idealism when dealing with nature and the environment in juxtaposition with industrial demands can be unhelpful. Climate Change is, above all things, apolitical and should not be tied to a particular party but to all parties. It is infinitely bigger than a fringe political group no matter how well intentioned. Peaceful civil demonstration must become the norm for all citizens. It must be world-wide and continuous not just for a few months but if necessary for years. Only this way will the more recalcitrant governments understand that they have to act. No matter how uncomfortable and potentially politically unpopular and destabilising it might feel, especially amongst those parties that enjoy an enhanced relationship with particular elements of 'big business', all this must be set aside for the benefit of humankind. In the final analysis, it is the voters who elect the government and unless they carry out their wishes, any comfortable industrial allegiance will be meaningless. There has never been a more important time to rally the world's whole population!

Chapter Sixteen
The Future of Humanity

There have been countless literary attempts to describe what humanity's terminal days might be like. Many of them were simply using 'the future' as a backdrop to their chosen storyline, but those that were referenced at the outset of this book were selected partly because of their popularity but also because they were woven around the idea of a plausible trajectory for humanity as seen by their authors at the time of writing. In some, there was also a more philosophical edge making a political statement, offering a warning of what might come to pass if the then current behaviours being witnessed were extrapolated and intensified.

Having now teased out the more obvious and immediate actions required to mitigate the effects of Climate Change and opined on their complexity and the likely uptake, there is enough data to draw up a picture of what the future world might look like. However, one of the complicating elements that emerged in early 2022 is Russia's invasion of Ukraine. There are two components to this, the first being Russia's extraordinary behaviour, a level of regression which has not been seen for more than 70 years and which most scholars of human behaviour had hoped was now something that could be consigned to history. The second is more straightforward, although extremely difficult to predict with any accuracy and that is simply what the physical outcome of the invasion will be. As an adjunct to that, the length of time that the war continues will have its own consequences.

In a worst case scenario there is the prospect for the use of nuclear weapons simply because the Russian leadership becomes overwhelmed with its lack of success and resorts to the use of the ultimate weapon. How the other nuclear powers of the world would react is hard to anticipate. It is possible, but highly unlikely, that there would be no nuclear response simply because the fallout from Russia's use of them in Ukraine would inevitably impact countries immediately adjacent and the sense of defilement would be profound. If the response was kept to a minimum then what would be Russia's response to a third party involving itself directly in its 'special military operation'? After all, Russia does not consider itself at war with Ukraine but simply cleaning up the 'Nazi elements' at work there. This is extremely dangerous territory as Russia could simply invent whatever background story it thought fit in order to justify its actions. In a limited exchange, a great deal of the land border between Ukraine and Russia would be rendered uninhabitable for both countries for the next fifty years or so. Nuclear fallout would spread across adjoining nations causing further long term restriction of land use and possible widespread sickness associated with the resulting radioactivity. The world would almost certainly be forced to put on hold much of what it was engaged on before the conflagration, obviously having a dramatic effect on the planning and execution of activities designed to mitigate the effects of Climate Change. If there was no retaliation by other nuclear powers, then the physical effects may be more limited. However, how the rest of the world would react to a one-sided nuclear escalation is very hard to predict. If its response was seen as nothing less than 'supine' then this may well encourage Russia to lift its aggression and aim for a wider spread of its authority throughout the Northern Hemisphere. Once again, Climate Change mitigation efforts would almost certainly stall in that environment and the prospect of a substantial shift in the power dynamic throughout the world could not be ruled out. This would be an ugly outcome, its consequences lasting well beyond the next fifty years. Images of George Orwell's *1984* must surely come to mind as being illustrative of the type of regime that a large part of the western world might find itself existing under.

If an initial nuclear exchange was to escalate and other nuclear powers joined the fray then much of Europe could become targets of Russian aggression while Russia herself would run the very real risk of being mortally damaged as a nation. Now, the picture might best be described by Nevil Shute's book *On the beach*. Here, there is no future as the radioactive fallout from a full scale nuclear exchange would cover the entire Northern Hemisphere quite quickly. The ensuing 'Nuclear winter', while throwing the current projected trajectory of Climate Change severely off-course, would have its own disastrous and largely terminal consequences for hundreds of millions of human beings. The weather systems of the planet would eventually carry the contamination to the greater part of the Southern Hemisphere as well. Humanity would reduce itself to a fraction of its current size and influence. The prospects for its long term survival would be severely challenged.

Nuclear war has been an existential threat since the invention of the atomic bomb and its subsequent use in 1945. Russia's invasion of Ukraine and its implied and actual threats not to discount the use of nuclear weapons in this war has simply brought the prospect into much sharper focus. As long as countries of the world have nuclear weapons, then the threat of their use will always remain. Remarkably, the very distributed ownership of such weapons across the Globe has resulted in something of a stalemate or stand-off. First use would almost certainly spark a retaliation which would in turn likely lead to further escalation. This stand-off has been effective for nearly 70 years. Now, however, the leadership of one superpower, whose relevance on the world stage has been waning of late, has shown that such restraint may no longer prevail.

To predict or imagine Humanity's future after a significant nuclear exchange between Russia, Europe and America is daunting. The images and consequences described by author and accomplished aeronautical engineer, Nevil Shute, are probably as close to reality as it is possible to predict.

It is sad to say that the thought processes which appear to lie behind Russia's behaviour and to which the rest of the world have been a privy to are not atypical of many sectors of humanity. The big difference with Russia is that these processes have spawned the execution of the most brutal and barbaric attack on a neighbouring country. The actions show up serious pathologies in the leaders who, although conducting their lives at a notionally high level, are demonstrating development in some areas which remain firmly fixed in the red meme or mythic/magic stage of human development. This is the level at which the school playground bully operates. Sadly, so many adults have enormous difficulty in advancing from this stage and will invariably revert to it during times of stress, often induced by outside challenges. Using their grasp of world politics combined with their ability to conduct many aspects of their lives at higher levels, the Russian leadership has created a storyline which in their minds gives them free reign over committing the most appalling atrocities on the civilian population of a neighbouring country which only 30 odd years ago was a part of the United Soviet Socialist Republic. These people were regarded by one and all as kindred Russians and yet today, because they have elected to take a different route in their country's development after leaving the USSR, they have been re-branded as Nazi collaborators. This exposes a tragic flaw in the underdeveloped human mind, one that earlier chapters have drawn attention to in the home, the workplace and at school. Mercifully, in these environments the pathologies associated with the lack of development only cause misery and hardship to family members, work colleagues and would-be school friends. Physical abuse is less common but when it does materialise then it arises from the same source. The tragedy for humanity is that these underdeveloped pathologically challenged members of the world society invariably find themselves in positions of absolute power. There is very little that humanity can do to help the individuals who are creating this chaos. Because of humanity's ability to operate at a relative high level of development in some areas while at the same time being incapable of behaving in like manner across the board, the result is a country leader who is quite comfortable with justifying brutality, murder and mayhem if he or she feels that this is an appropriate course of action which fits the storyline. Any hope of offering the subject counselling to help them manage these behaviours is out of the question simply because of the apparent level of development they have reached which allows them to occupy a position of seniority and authority which makes them effectively untouchable. In an autocratic society, there is no chance of their more enlightened peers, always assuming they have any, being able to offer them help. And so when a country has been driven into such a bleak corner with such distressingly dysfunctional leadership at the helm, the recovery process is a long and bleak one.

Depending on the developmental and operating level of the observer, Russia's behaviour has not elicited a common response. Instead there has been a wide range of comment and opinion offered, everything from total support all the way through to absolute indignation and contempt that a world leader could behave in this way, especially when the world is still reeling from the effects of a world-wide pandemic while looking straight down the barrel of an environmental disaster, the size and extent of which is still uncertain. The sovereign nations that are not involved with the conflict have shown constraint. Those that support Ukraine and are incensed over Russia's barbaric behaviour have resisted the temptation to escalate the conflict by joining in. The reasons for this are legion. Instead they have elected to help passively by assisting with the arming of Ukraine and the application of a range of economic sanctions against Russia. They stand accused by Russia of their own crimes by these actions but so far Russia has resisted the temptation to draw them into its 'military operation' by attacking them. Those that appear to or who actually support Russia are following a similar protocol, although there is limited evidence of the supply of arms to Russia to assist with its operation. Instead, the support is through rhetoric alone. There is a distinct effort by most states to stay out of the conflict. Despite the vigorous condemnation on one hand and the vocal support being offered on the other, there is no appetite to join the fray largely because of the very real fear of a rapid escalation. Sadly, this inaction will be viewed by many as being weak on the one side or passively complicit on the other. It would be heartening if the main reason could be construed as an attempt to assist with the solution of a third party conflict at a higher developmental level than using a physical assault. This is something that Ukraine was never given the opportunity to do as Russia launched an unannounced and unprovoked attack on the country, with the simple explanation that it was just a 'special military operation'. The opportunity for discussion and negotiation was never provided, the least complex reason being that Russia had convinced itself that it was acting in good faith in accordance with the background story that it had told itself. Despite all of this, the abiding sentiment that should be taken away from the invasion is the measured way that the remainder of the world has behaved towards it. The situation could have become so much worse if the response had been along the lines of the Second World War, although the circumstances surrounding the outbreak were very much more complex.

Fortunately for humankind, the picture is not all bleak. There are many millions of humans across the Globe who will welcome guidance from family, peers, friends and other sources. These will be the engines that will drive humanity's fight for survival. They have the opportunity to make real progress in spite of the woeful examples being set by many of the world's leaders. To coin a Trade Union inspired battle cry, the energy source for change must come from the 'grass roots' of society the world over. It is from here that the momentum must be built by sensitive, empathetic action, by peaceful demonstration, by constantly challenging those in authority to publicise targets and progress. Only when the world is heartily sick of the constant rumblings of public discontent will action begin to be second nature. By then more and more people will have understood the need to raise their levels of personal spiritual development and will have acted accordingly. If these numbers are big enough they may be sufficient to enact wholesale change across the Globe and humankind can really claim to have left behind the archaic practises and behaviours which have dogged it for thousands of years. Erica Chenoweth and her colleague have settled on the requisite figure of 3.5% of the population to initiate change. That amounts to 245 million World inhabitants, not that far off the population of America. Because of the very wide number of establishments and institutions that need to be convinced of the necessity of change, that number may be inadequate. If that is the case, and the critical mass turns out to be much higher, then its achievement may be beyond humanity. That will leave a world struggling with the effects of Climate Change and still underperforming individually when compared with what it should be possible to achieve.

The cataclysmic consequences of being unable to control mean earthly temperature rise are a matter for conjecture. There is an argument that temperatures will continue to rise without restraint once a certain critical tipping point has been reached. This would surely lead to the world ceasing to be habitable in many places. Sea level rise would be measured in tens of metres instead of centimetres. The drowning of crop yielding lands so necessary for supporting the population would be widespread. Insect populations would be decimated and the knock-on effects would be felt world-wide. Whether humanity could survive such an apocalypse is hard to determine. The earth and its inhabitants would be hardly recognisable compared with today's picture. Of course, none of this would happen overnight. There would be plenty of time for humanity to play its time-worn card, that of blame. Maybe that would lead to one group confronting another with the other time-worn option, physical violence. It is difficult to envisage anything other than terminal decay from that point on.

On the other hand, maybe the magic percentage is reached and humankind is able to follow some sort of practical path which does end up restricting mean temperature rise and perhaps, more importantly, actually halting it. There will still be massive global changes; sea levels will have risen, much land will have been inundated, the climate will no longer sustain habitation by humans or other animals in many locations around the world, the ability to feed a population as it is today will not be there which will result in widespread famine and death. Again, the time-worn antidotes of blame and violence will probably rise up and there will be widespread hostility. In this scenario, because a significant portion of the population has been able to raise its own level of development, the battles may be contained and a majority could learn to live and work together in some measure of harmony. Whether that is sustainable long term would again be a matter for conjecture but the prognosis must have improved because humanity has broadened its discovery of some of the higher levels of personal development and has begun operating at those levels.

It would be disingenuous not to point out that all of the current challenges facing humankind are of its own making. There is no greater power that can be pointed at and blamed or attacked physically to claim some sort of retribution. Not surprisingly, all the solutions or ameliorating actions are also in humanity's control. It has the engineering and scientific ability to reinvent the technology that it has come to depend on to be less offensive to the environment, it can modify the way it abuses it and its fellow beings and it can concentrate on raising its levels of development such that a larger number of souls can live in harmony with one another. It can address all of these things in concert or it can take a piecemeal approach and address only those things which will inconvenience the status quo the least amount. Alternatively, it can be completely distracted by other earthly matters, such as war, elections, international bickering between sovereign states, or simply hanging on to the material riches and status that it has achieved and as a result, do absolutely nothing. In one direction, lies the opportunity to reduce the predicted impact of Global Warming and to give humanity a possible last chance to improve its behaviour while in the other direction it seems that it is bent on a painfully slow but inevitable terminal decay. Will humankind now embrace the changes so desperately needed and so long identified by the Ancient philosophers and echoed down through the ages by their successors to the present day? This is the real question regarding our survival; the relatively small practicalities of responding to Climate Change are modest by comparison. The choice is ours to make.

References

Chapter One

1. George Orwell. 8 June 1949. 'Nineteen eighty-four'. Publisher, Secker and Warburg, London, United Kingdom.
2. Ray Bradbury. 19 October 1953. 'Fahrenheit 451'. Published by Ballantine Books, United States of America.
3. Kazuo Ishiguro. 5 April 2005. 'Never let me go'. Published by Faber and Faber, London, United Kingdom.
4. James Lovelock and Bryan Appleyard. 4 July 1919. 'Novacene'. Published by Penguin Books/Allen Lane, London, United Kingdom.
5. Aldous Huxley. 1932. 'Brave New World'. Published by Chatto and Windus, London, United Kingdom.
6. Harry Harrison. 1966. 'Make room! Make room!' formed the basis of the film 'Soylent Green' released in May 1973, directed by Richard Fleischer, distributed by Metro-Goldwyn-Mayer, United States of America.
7. Story by Adam McKay and David Sirota.fC The film *Don't Look Up*. Released in December 2021. Directed by Adam McKay, United States of America.
8. Nevil Shute. 1957. 'On the Beach'. Published by Heinemann, United Kingdom.

Chapter Two

1. IPCC Working Group 1 report. Climate Change 2021: The Physical Science Basis. Contribution of Working Group I to the Sixth Assessment Report of the Intergovernmental Panel on Climate Change. 9 August 2021.

2. Thomas Newcomen. Prosser, R.B. "Thomas Newcomen (1663–1729)." Dictionary of National Biography Volume 40 Myllar—Nicholls. Ed. Lee, Sidney. London: Smith, Elder & Co., 1894. 326–29.

Chapter Three

1. Oxford University Museum of Natural History. 'The history of life in a single year'. Copyright © 2006.
2. Australian electricity options: pumped hydro energy storage. 20 July 2020. Professor Andrew Blakers, Dr Matthew Stocks and Bin LuAustralian National University.
3. TIMES Progress and prospects of thermo-mechanical energy storage—a critical review by Andreas V. Olympios et al. Progress in Energy, 12 March 2021.
4. CAES. M.K.C. Donev et al. (2018). Energy Education—Compressed air energy storage [Online]. Available
5. https://energyeducation.ca/encyclopedia/Compressed_air_energy_sto rage. [Accessed: July 24, 2022].
6. The 5,298MW Belchatow power plant located in Poland is the biggest coal-fired power plant in Europe. Operational since 1988, the plant is owned and operated by PGE Elektrownia Belchatow (PGE), a subsidiary of state-owned Polska Grupa Energetyczna (PGE). https://www.nsenergybusiness.com

Chapter Four

1. Justine Lovell. Australian Energy Council. 30 January 2020.
2. "EVS: are they really more efficient?" Melbourne, Victoria, Australia.
3. Visual Capitalist. Govind Bhutada. 28 February 2022. "Mapped: EV Battery Manufacturing Capacity, by Region". Vancouver, B.C.

Chapter Five

1. The Destruction of Pompeii, 79 AD, "Eye Witness to History, www.eyewitnesstohistory.com (1999)
2. "The Great Smog of 1952". metoffice.gov.uk.

Chapter Six

1. Ken Wilber, "Sex, Ecology and Spirituality", page 198, Figure 5.1 'Some details of the Four Quadrants'. Shambhala Publications, Boulder, Colorado, USA, Second edition 2000.
2. Yuval Noah Harari, Penguin, Random House, UK 2014. 'Sapiens', Page 38.

Chapter Seven

1. Plato's "Republic". Translated by Christopher Rowe. Published by Penguin Books, 2012.
2. Plato's "Republic". Page 230 to Page 239. Translated by Christopher Rowe. Published by Penguin Books, 2012.
3. Plato's "Republic". Page 239 to Page 244. Translated by Christopher Rowe. Published by Penguin Books, 2012.

Chapter Eight

1. Yuval Noah Harari, Penguin, Random House, UK 2014. 'Sapiens'
2. Ken Wilber, "Sex, Ecology and Spirituality", page 198, Figure 5.1 'Some details of the Four Quadrants'. Shambhala Publications, Boulder, Colorado, USA, Second edition, 2000.
3. Alexander Pope. "An essay on Criticism". 1709, UK.

Chapter Nine

1. Ken Wilber. "A Theory of Everything" Page 5. Shambhala, Boulder, Colorado, USA. Published 2001.
2. Ken Wilbur. "A Theory of Everything" Page 5. Shambhala, Boulder, Colorado, USA. Published 2001.
3. Ken Wilbur. "A Theory of Everything" Page 5. Shambhala, Boulder, Colorado, USA. Published 2001.
4. Ken Wilber. "A Theory of Everything" Page 7–13. Shambhala, Boulder, Colorado, USA. Published 2001.

5. Margaret Mahler. Born 1897. Died 1985. Austrian/American psychiatrist who pioneered work in child development.

6. Ken Wilber, "Sex, Ecology and Spirituality", pages 45–46, Introduction to the 'Kosmos'. Shambhala Publications, Boulder, Colorado, USA, Second edition, 2000.

7. Ken Wilber, "Sex, Ecology and Spirituality", page 198, Figure 5.1 'Some details of the Four Quadrants'. Shambhala Publications, Boulder, Colorado, USA, Second edition, 2000.

8. Ken Wilber, "Sex, Ecology and Spirituality", pages 23 to 25. Hierarchy. Shambhala Publications, Boulder, Colorado, USA, Second Edition, 2000.

9. Ken Wilber, "Sex, Ecology and Spirituality", pages17 to 25. General Systems Theory and resolution of Hierarchy Inconsistencies. Shambhala Publications, Boulder, Colorado, USA. Second Edition, 2000.

10. Ken Wilber, "Sex, Ecology and Spirituality", page 23. Hierarchy. Shambhala Publications, Boulder, Colorado, USA, Second Edition, 2000.

11. Ken Wilber, "Sex, Ecology and Spirituality", page 25. Hierarchy. Shambhala Publications, Boulder, Colorado, USA, Second Edition, 2000.

12. Ken Wilber, "A Theory of Everything". Page 9. Shambhala Publications, Boulder, Colorado, USA, Published 2001.

13. Ken Wilber, "A Theory of Everything". Page 20. Shambhala Publications, Boulder, Colorado, USA, Published 2001.

Chapter Ten

1. Ken Wilber, "A Theory of Everything". Pages 41 and 86. Flatland. Shambhala Publications, Boulder, Colorado, USA, Published, 2001.

2. Ken Wilber, "Sex, Ecology and Spirituality". Page 139. Interior versus Exterior. Shambhala Publications, Boulder, Colorado, USA, Second Edition, 2000.

3. Ken Wilber, "Sex, Ecology and Spirituality". Pages 83–84. Omega Point. Shambhala Publications, Boulder, Colorado, USA, Second Edition, 2000.

4. Ken Wilber, "Sex, Ecology and Spirituality". Page 84. Omega Point according to Piaget. Shambhala Publications, Boulder, Colorado, USA, Second Edition, 2000.

5. Ken Wilber, "Sex, Ecology and Spirituality". Page 84. Omega Point according to Habermas. Shambhala Publications, Boulder, Colorado, USA, Second Edition, 2000.

6. Ken Wilber, "A Theory of Everything". The Yellow meme. Pages 12–13. Shambhala Publications, Boulder, Colorado, USA, Published, 2001.

7. Ken Wilber, "A Theory of Everything". The Turquoise meme. Page 13. Shambhala Publications, Boulder, Colorado, USA, Published, 2001.

8. Einstein. Part of a letter of commiseration to a grieving father, Robert S Marcus in February 1950. The Marginalian. Einstein Widening our Circle of Compassion. Maria Popova.

Chapter Eleven

1. Marcus Aurelius. 121 A.D. Meditations. Translated by A.S.I Farquharson. MacMillan Collector's Library.

Chapter Thirteen

1. Erica Chenoweth is an assistant professor at the Josef Korbel School of International Studies at the University of Denver and an Associate Senior Researcher at the Peace Research Institute of Oslo. Previously she taught at Wesleyan University and held fellowships at Harvard, Stanford, and the University of California at Berkeley.

2. Maria J. Stephan is a strategic planner with the U.S. Department of State. Formerly she served as director of policy and research at the International Centre on Nonviolent Conflict (ICNC) and as an adjunct professor at Georgetown University and American University. She has also been a fellow at the Kennedy School of Government's Belfer Centre for Science and International Affairs.

3. Erica Chenoweth and Maria J. Stephan. Why Civil Resistance Works: The Strategic Logic of Nonviolent Conflict (New York, NY: Columbia University Press, August 2011).

4. Columbia University Press. Summary of publication "Why Civil Resistance Works: The Strategic Logic of Nonviolent Conflict". Erica Chenoweth and Maria J. Stephan. Columbia University Press, August 2011.

Chapter Fourteen

1. Ken Wilber, "A Theory of Everything". Pages 7–8. Shambhala Publications, Boulder, Colorado, USA, Published 2001.

Chapter Fifteen

1. Hugh Van Cuylenburg. 'The Resilience Project'. Chapter Four. 'Discovering Happiness'. Ebury Press 2019.

www.ingramcontent.com/pod-product-compliance
Lightning Source LLC
Chambersburg PA
CBHW060510290526

45791CB00001B/343